HOW TO GIVE
A
SPEECH

Winifred Marks

INSTITUTE OF PERSONNEL MANAGEMENT

Cartoons in the text by Martin Hegley

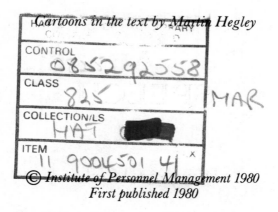

© *Institute of Personnel Management 1980*
First published 1980

Printed in Great Britain by Lonsdale Universal
Printing Ltd

ISBN 0 85292 255 8

CONTENTS

FOREWORD

General aims
This book is intended to help anyone faced with making a speech, in a lecture hall, at a business meeting, to a club or society, to the general public, on a social occasion or even as a test. Some may be born orators but many more have oratory thrust upon them. Inexperienced speakers in particular tend to worry about what to say and how to say it. Their anxiety is understandable. It arises basically from a lack of confidence.

To be asked to make a speech is a compliment. It implies that the speaker has some worthwhile knowledge of the subject and that he can present it in a way which will interest and edify the audience. The speaker is anxious to justify this opinion by sharing his knowledge but does not wish to run any risk of appearing dogmatic or conceited. He wants the audience to benefit from his speech and to enjoy listening to it, without becoming bored or thinking they could be spending their time more profitably in the library or the bar.

He feels a responsibility towards those who have

asked him to speak and wishes to be a credit to them. If he is speaking as a representative of a group, a club, a school, a company or even the government, he is acutely conscious that the reputation of the organization may be enhanced or diminished by his performance.

He is also concerned to protect himself from possible criticism. Most speakers are aware of the old adage that it it better to say nothing and be thought a fool than to speak and prove that one is.

In our day to day dealings most of us find speaking easier than writing. At ease among our friends we express ourselves fluently and with the humour, force and turns of phrase that clarify our meaning and express our personality. We repeat and rephrase our ideas, we give examples and illustrations, we watch reactions and check by questioning until we are sure the message has been correctly understood.

On being asked to give a speech, however, many of us become apprehensive and diffident. Standing in front of an audience evokes in us feelings more appropriate to an early Christian saint facing a hostile mob on Chesil Bank. Our nervousness makes us defensive. We repress spontaneity and individuality. We concentrate on reason and logic and distrust emotion. Our language becomes impersonal and cold, our demeanour stiff and unapproachable. Waning self-confidence and growing self-consciousness lead us to concentrate all our attention on ourselves and on what we are saying to the exclusion of the needs and even the readily observable reactions of the audience.

A moment's reflection reveals this fear as largely imaginary. Hardly any speakers suffer physical damage or even indignity at the hands of their audiences, few of whom come ready provided with rotting vegetables. Speakers who are roughly treated are almost invariably politicians or sociologists known in advance to hold extremist and unpopular views.

Words can harm us, whatever the proverb says, but the risk of mental injury is slight and the potential rewards great. A good speech earns the whole-hearted approval of the audience and gives great satisfaction to the speaker, the satisfaction of an intellectual achievement and social acclaim. It may produce some tangible result for the sponsors, perhaps an increase in membership of an organization or a club, or an improvement in work performance. It may even earn the speaker a worthwhile fee and/or a free trip and a good meal. A few people regularly supplement their income by undertaking paid speech engagements.

The fear of making a speech can only be overcome by making one successfully and experiencing the rewards. Good results cannot be guaranteed but problems can be minimized by following a planned approach based on thorough preparation. A great deal of uncertainty can be eliminated beforehand. Any speaker can gain confidence through the knowledge that his speech contains good material, that he will not dry up and that he will not antagonize the audience.

What is a speech?

The type of speech considered here is an address to a number of people, for which the speaker is given time free from interruptions to make a statement. It is not a chat between friends or colleagues, nor an open discussion.

It is an honest attempt to impart information and

views in a manner which the audience will readily accept and perhaps even enjoy.

While the speaker's personal interpretation of the content is not only inevitable but desirable, the speech should not deliberately distort evidence. It should not exclude all the facts contrary to the speaker's line of argument and thereby give a falsely pessimistic or optimistic intepretation of the real position. It is not a call to arms, a political manifesto or a travel brochure.

A speech has to command the interest of the audience. One composed solely of concrete facts and figures, presented without humour or any appeal to

the emotions would soon fall on deaf ears. Light relief helps to engage and retain attention. On the other hand a continuous flow of jokes unrelated to an underlying serious theme is not a speech but a comedian's patter.

The aim is an interesting exposition of an honest and well balanced sequence of information and ideas.

Why make a speech?

We may be called upon to give a speech for reasons which make it difficult or downright impossible to refuse. It may form part of our job. The obvious examples in this category are appeals officers of charitable institutions and university lecturers but few escape the occasional talk given in the line of duty. Personnel managers give careers talks to assembled school-leavers, present reports at meetings of the board and participation committees. Even accountants are now flushed out of their offices to explain the company's accounts in simple terms to managers and workers' representatives so that they can make suggestions about improving profitability.

Sometimes we are impelled to take the initiative in speaking to a group of colleagues or subordinates in order to effect a change in working methods. This often happens when conditions change within the organization. The extended use of the computer radically changed systems of stock control in shops and factories, record-keeping and office routine everywhere. Many meetings had to be held to explain the changes and the reasons for them, allay fears of mass redundancy and generally prevent breakdown of the organization and of the employees affected.

Sometimes we are driven to speak out of concern

for the public good. We may feel so strongly, for example, about the way the rates are being squandered or lack of adequate laboratory facilities at our children's school, that we call and address a public meeting.

Other causes of launching into speech-making are:

by specific invitation
by officiating or being the guest of honour at a social or educational function
training needs
selection procedures.

If you are known to be a collector of Victorian mechanical toys or an ex-chorister of Westminster Abbey, you are likely to be in demand to address the Townswomen's Guild or the local music club. Such invitations are difficult to refuse without appearing churlish, especially if the choice of dates is every other Thursday afternoon between 15 September and 12 April.

Any one of us is liable to be called upon, often at short notice, to say a few words on behalf of the group presenting a gift to X who has completed 25 years' service, Y who is retiring or marrying (or both) or Z who has won the Founder's Prize for creative thought. If we happen to be X, Y or Z we are expected to make a suitable reply.

Some organizations realize that their managers will be required to make speeches in the course of their careers and deliberately set out to train them to speak well before an audience. An essential part of this training is practice, which might nowadays be before a television camera.

A few organizations include an impromptu or prepared speech (or both) as part of their selection procedure for graduates and/or managers.

One way and another it is increasingly hard to find a specialist, a manager or a knowledgeable amateur in any field of general interest who has not been called upon to make a speech, give a talk or explain something at length before an audience.

If you have any option about accepting an invitation to speak, do not take it up lightly. It takes time to prepare a good speech and no one wishes to give a bad one. Not only is the speaker's own reputation at stake; in agreeing to speak he undertakes some obligation to the audience to reward their patience (or long-suffering) by making the most effective speech of which he is capable.

If you genuinely lack the time to prepare, it is better for everyone if you decline gracefully. It is only courteous to give an adequate reason and suggest an alternative speaker, if possible, after ascertaining that he is able and willing.

(*Author's note:* I am particularly aware that speakers may be women and that some of the best in fact are. For the sake of convenience and style, I have used the convention whereby *he* also means *she* whenever the context is appropriate.)

Part I
HOW TO PREPARE A SPEECH

BACKGROUND INFORMATION

Before agreeing to give a speech you need certain basic information. Do not take at its face value a casual invitation to say a few words about your trip to the West Indies to the boys at the Station Hotel next week. You may be confronted as expected by the rugby team and its supporters in a relaxed mood after the match or by leading naturalists from four neighbouring counties agog to hear all about the flora and fauna. The audience may be lounging in the bar with pint pots in their hands or sitting in formal rows in the conference hall. They may wish to interrupt your travellers' tales with romantic memories of their own or ask erudite questions after you have finished. It is difficult to imagine a basic speech which would adequately cover both eventualities.

The subject and the audience

First be clear about your subject. It is not only general topics like holidays or declining standards which are capable of various interpretations. Talks on biscuits given to the Mothers' Union, the Institute of Packaging and a group of PhDs in food technology would scarcely be recognizable as covering the same subject, or so it may be hoped.

The composition of the audience obviously makes a great deal of difference to the content of the speech, to its style and to the method of presentation. It is inadvisable to accept an invitation, let alone to start writing down your ideas, before you know whether the audience is composed of:

experts, enthusiastic amateurs or beginners with little or no knowledge of the subject

volunteers attending in their own time or a group selected by their teachers, employers, nurses or warders

mixed age groups and sexes or a specific group (eg under-graduates, middle-aged women, schoolchildren, the Darby and Joan Club).

If you have been invited to speak, it is because someone believes you have something useful or at least interesting to tell a particular group of people. This could be an unfounded belief. If you know less about the subject than the majority of the expected audience or if you are not genuinely interested in it, refuse the invitation. It is kinder to the audience and better for your reputation.

On the other hand do not be bashful because of a lack of academic qualifications when you have good practical experience and first-hand knowledge of the subject. One of the most interesting speakers on ornithology is a man without a letter after his name, whose love of birds glows in every sentence and shines through every photograph. Sometimes practical experience is exactly what an academic audience wishes to hear about, as when management students invite a supervisor or a shop steward to speak about industrial relations on the shop floor.

There may be times when you know little about the subject but are nevertheless the best choice of speaker. It could be vital to convey information quickly about which others have even less knowledge or ability to absorb it and pass it on. This might happen if anti-radiation drill has to be explained to heads of households in a hurry and you are a community fire officer or the head of a local school. A more likely example (with any luck) might occur when your organization installs an internal telephone system and sends written instructions on how to operate it to managers, who must explain it to all their staff.

In these circumstances you have no choice. Accept without demur and do the best you can.

The time

Another essential piece of information you need before accepting an invitation to speak is when and where the speech is to be given. If it is in Glasgow at 7 pm on a day when you are winding up a conference in Torquay at 4 pm you must decline.

In other situations the issue is not as clear cut. The talk may be somewhere local in a month's time on a day on which you are quite free. You must decide whether this allows adequate time for the preparation. How much work will be needed?

are you used to preparing speeches?
is the topic new to you as a speaker?
is the material readily available?
can you get help in obtaining the information you
    will need?

can you get help in interpreting material and in presentation?

can your secretary get background information, eg about the audience, the venue, the chairman and other speakers?

What are your previous commitments?

is any time available during the working day or between lessons and lectures?

does the speech warrant spending your employer's time on it or neglecting other studies or putting off routine chores for a time?

have you any spare time at week-ends or in the evenings?

does your free time coincide with the opening hours of sources of information, eg reference libraries?

will unexpected commitments at work, at school or college, or at home take priority or can you guarantee a certain number of hours' preparation?

If you have no choice and the date is uncomfortably close, then time should be allocated as a priority. Compulsion usually denotes that the speech is part of the speaker's job or essential voluntary duties, which justifies using the time required. In extreme cases, hiding in a library incognito may be advisable.

The place

In order to plan your speech to advantage you also need to know the type of room in which you will speak:

is it small or large?

where will you stand or sit to speak?

how is it furnished for the speaker and the audience?

how good are the acoustics?

what temperature controls are available?

is there likely to be noise inside or outside the building?

If you intend to use visual aids or sound effects you must also find out:

what equipment is available

how many electric points there are, where they are placed and whether they are of the correct voltage.

If defects are revealed, some can be rectified. You can ask for a microphone, different seating arrangements or a lectern. You can take your own slide projector or adaptor plugs or change the speech to do without the film or slides you had in mind. You could wear a woollen vest or a thin cotton dress to combat extremes of temperature.

One word of caution: if the speech is to be given in some distant place, travelling expenses and accommodation are usually offered. It is as well to check this to avoid the possibility of being put to considerable expense. You also need to know what arrangements (if any) have been made to feed you before or after the meeting and who is the host. It is embarrassing to be faced with a three-course dinner when you have already dined and could be even more embarrassing to find you are paying for the unwanted meal. Sometimes speakers are expected to remain after the meeting to meet the hosts and members socially and/or to drink together, a crucial matter for drivers. To plan your journey home, you must find out how long these festivities are expected to last and whether anyone will drive you to the station if you are without a car.

Arrive in good time

At whatever time of day your speech is due to start, allow plenty of time to make sure you arrive early. If you are travelling by public transport, do not set out to catch the last possible train or 'bus but an earlier one. If the place is many miles away and you are driving yourself, allow an average speed of 50 mph on motorways and 30 mph on other roads and then time for mishaps. If you are unfamiliar with the building in which you are going to speak, ask the chairman for a map and allow extra time for asking directions of strangers to the district and coping with unfamiliar one-way traffic systems.

Many institutions have parking spaces which are inadequate, carefully concealed and available only to those who can produce the right password or permit. Find out beforehand what the arrangements are so that you can arrive armed with a written authority if necessary. It makes all the difference to your timing (and your state of mind) to be ushered by a commissionaire with a smile into a reserved space in front of the building rather than to be scowlingly denied entry and have to drive frantically round the district to find a space in a side street half a mile away and worry all the evening about vandalism.

It is not conducive to a relaxed, confident frame of mind to spend the last hour of the journey in terror of arriving late. To be late is also discourteous to one's host and the audience, who may themselves have made considerable efforts to arrive on time.

You need to be early also to greet the chairman, check the seating and equipment, wash and brush up and generally make yourself at home.

ASSEMBLING MATERIAL

When you have agreed the subject of the speech, when you know the make-up of the audience and the conditions in which you will speak, you are ready to start preparing the material.

Most speakers have a great deal of information about their subjects from academic sources and/or practical experience. At worst they are the people with the best prospect of understanding the reasons for whatever change is advocated (eg the necessity to adopt metric weights and measures) and translating written instructions into the raw material of effective action.

Where to find the facts

An honours degree followed by a lifetime of experience does not in itself, however, constitute a speech. Most speakers need to glean material from a number of sources. Once the subject has been settled, it is amazing how many references to it will spring to the eye and the ear in newspapers and magazines, on the wireless and television. Cut them out or jot them down on the spot before they become hazy in the mind. If the cutting is taken from the centre of a page, remember to write on it the date and the name of the publication. If the information has been heard on the wireless or television, again note the date and the source, the author or the government paper. It is infuriating to have collected a note giving just the statistic you need to make a telling point and then to be unable to use it because it cannot be verified.

Books are an obvious source of information and libraries an obvious source of books. Many large companies have their own technical libraries, staffed by experts. They are often prepared to supply information on technical matters concerning their products

and manufacturing processes. You could with justi-fication enquire for instance about closed circuit tele-vision equipment if you had to speak about advanced training methods or shoplifting.

Central reference libraries in cities and reference sections of any good library employ trained staff who are glad to help serious enquirers. When consulting a central library, it is indeed advisable to be specific in your requests to avoid disappearing under a mountain of documents. As well as getting out books, Acts of Parliament, statistical tables and other light reading matter for you to consult, the staff will look up the answers to concrete questions such as 'What were the annual increases in the cost of living between 1950 and 1978?'

Government departments from the Treasury to the Department of Social Security are gold mines of information and put out hundreds of helpful leaflets explaining in simple terms difficult matters, such as the real national income and how to claim a rates rebate.

It is neither hard nor complicated to approach them. They are willing and indeed anxious to help the public (contrary to popular opinion) and to clarify and disseminate the facts which they are in a unique position to collect and interpret. Part of their role is educational. If what you ask for is 'top secret', of course, you will be advised (as they say) firmly and politely.

Their addresses and telephone numbers are given in local directories or can be obtained from reference libraries or branch offices of the ministry concerned. When making an enquiry by telephone or in writing it pays to be specific about the information sought. If the organization is large enough, there will be a section which deals with enquiries. If not, your letter or call will be passed on to the appropriate person to answer. In dealing with any large organization, it is wise to make a note of the name and telephone extension of the person who deals with you, in case you wish to follow up any points later.

There may be times when a personal visit is considered preferable, either because time is short or you are unsure about how much information is available or likely to be forthcoming. All government offices have a receptionist, ranging from the typist nearest the door in a small office to a uniformed janitor or two in an imposing booth barring the entrance to a ministry. Be prepared to state your business clearly and intelligibly on the well founded assumption that the receptionist will be willing and able to help you find the right person to give you the answers. It helps if you present yourself dressed in a way which does not give rise to suspicions of spying or anarchy and without any bulky packages. No receptionist wishes to be the one who admitted the saboteur.

The other difficulty of making an unannounced visit is that you may find you have come to the wrong office or that the material you need will take several days to prepare. A preliminary telephone call or letter often smoothes the way and saves time in the long run.

Check the facts
Make sure you are familiar with the general background of your subject and make a permanent note of the most important names, events and dates. Facts, figures and quotations should always be verified and

written down in a convenient form for later reference. Even if you do not use them in the speech or refer to them only to support a line of argument, they could be invaluable at question time or for future talks.

Memory is fickle. How many can quote accurately the next line to Thomas Mordaunt's

One crowded hour of glorious life ?*

Gather illustrative material from your own and other people's experience. Friends and colleagues are usually more than willing to provide a wealth of anecdotes on anything from laying crazy paving to winning the last trade war.

The diligent researcher's difficulty becomes an embarrassment of riches but it is easier to discard what is irrelevant or of secondary importance and speak from a store of undisclosed knowledge than to spin out 15 minutes' material into half an hour's talk.

* It goes on: 'Is worth an age without a name'

THE FRAMEWORK

Theme and treatment
An effective speech has a single, consistent main theme. The speaker explains and develops the theme in whatever depth fits in with the needs and interests of the audience and the time at his disposal. There are usually several subsections exploring different aspects of the topic.

It has three basic sections:

Introduction
    a statement of the main theme
    reference to the content of the sub-sections
Development
    detailed treatment of the theme
        and/by means of
    detailed treatment of every sub-section
Conclusion
    summary of the line of the main argument
    clarification of the purpose, stressing the means
    of fulfilling it.

In the development section, every major heading has its own framework ie introduction, development (supported by facts and illustrated from experience) and summary. Transitions from one section to the next should be made smoothly, indicating their relevance to the main theme.

A simple, logical framework is essential:

to clarify the speaker's own ideas

to facilitate the logical development of the theme

to enable the speaker to assemble relevant material efficiently

to ensure that no important aspect of the subject is omitted

to help the speaker remember the speech as he delivers it

to enable the audience to follow the main line of argument easily and to remember the most important points.

Examples

It may be helpful to consider as examples the framework of three different speeches.

Example 1
Title: Let's start knitting!
Purpose: To encourage the group to start knitting or to improve their knitting for their own satisfaction, economic reasons and charitable purposes.
Main theme: The advantages to be gained from simple as well as advanced knitting.
This talk could be illustrated by showing patterns, samplers, finished garments, blankets and so on.

INTRODUCTION
Definition of knitting and brief history of its development. Outline scope for all knitters (beginners to

experts) to exercise skill, choice and discrimination.

Brief statement of uses

    clothing—warmth, style and comfort
    blankets and other covers
    carpets and wall hangings
    decorations, eg cushion covers, lacy edging.

Patterns

    getting the right size and style for the garment (or
        other end product) bearing in mind the needs
        and preferences of the recipient
    checking tension to ensure correct measurements
        and changing the size of the needles if necessary
    using different stitches to make the work
        more or less bulky
        warmer or cooler
        plainer or more fancy
        easier or more interesting
    using different yarns.

Yarns

    yarns available
        wool
        cotton
        man-made fibres, eg nylon, courtelle, rayon
        mixtures of natural and man-made fibres
    their strengths and weaknesses
        warmth
        durability
        washing properties
        elasticity
        shape retention
        creasing

24

thickness of yarn in relation to needles and density
of finished fabric
problems of using yarns in different materials or
colours.

Stitches
plain and purl and their derivatives
garter stitch
stocking stitch
ribbing—single, double, transposed etc
moss stitch
patterns made by using mixtures of plain and purl
stitches eg
blocks of reversed stocking stitch
diamond shapes
ridges of garter stitch in stocking stitch
cable stitches and their derivatives
cables on four or more stitches
false cables
twisting stitches forward and back
bobbles eg blackberry stitch
Aran patterns
Fair Isle
mixing colours
carrying the yarns along
preventing bunching or looseness.

Professional finish
pressing
seams for different sections
binding
backing

CONCLUSION
Reasons for knitting

limitless choice, compared with range in shops
a congenial occupation, affording great satisfaction
    as the work takes shape and scope for creativity
an economical hobby with great potential savings
    (mistakes can be rectified and old work reknitted)
opportunity to help others and/or to earn a little.

Ways of helping others and oneself
    saving on knitted shop garments
    re-using old knitting
    becoming a professional knitter
    squares for blankets for refugees
    baby clothes for needy mothers
    garments for charity sales.

Take names of those willing to help and note what they
    are prepared to do.

Example 2
Title: Make good use of your library.
Purpose: To introduce small groups of children aged 10
    to 12 to the facilities offered by the library and
    show them how to use it.
Main theme: The range of books available and how to
    find what is wanted.
This talk should take place in the library to groups of
not more than eight children and be illustrated by
showing the books and the system.

INTRODUCTION
The library is an exciting place, packed full of interest.
No need to wait for:
    annuals at Christmas
    television programmes to follow the adventures of
        the Muppets, Starsky and Hutch, Tom and Jerry

26

your father to show you how to make a model aero-
plane fly

anyone to tell you how to spell a word in a letter or
homework.

Help yourself in the library!

Fiction and how to find it
alphabetical arrangement by author on shelves
how to find other books by the same author if pleased
with one
indexes of authors and titles
markers on the back of books eg D for detection, A for
adventure, SF for science fiction, W for westerns
how to order a book that is out on loan
how to suggest a book that is not in stock.

Hobbies
how to find books on model making, cricket, tennis,
football, knitting, cookery and so on
simple description of classification system
music books (singing, playing, opera librettos)
getting help from the library staff.

Study
how to find information and answers for homework and projects eg history, geography, natural
history
English and foreign languages
grammar
literature
reference books
dictionaries: English, foreign, specialist
encyclopedias
Roget's Thesaurus

27

where to find them
how to use them
rules about removing books
working in the library.

General interest
art and picture books
plays and poetry
humour
newspapers, magazines and other periodicals.

CONCLUSION
The library is a treasure house full of books to read
for pleasure
to advance skills and hobbies
to help with studies.
It can be freely and easily used. The staff are there to
help you.
Issue borrowers' tickets. General information on
length of loans and fines.

Example 3
Title: Why do managers join trade unions?
Purpose: To explain to the directors of several small
companies within a large group why 90 per cent
of their managers joined an independent,
company-based trade union.
Main theme: The deteriorating fortunes of managers
during the 1970s especially when compared with
other income groups.

INTRODUCTION
Growth in membership of management unions in
general and of the company union in particular.

28

Development of the company management union from a social club to an independent, certificated trade union.

Summary of reasons for this under the headings:

> the good old days of the 1960s
> effects of successive governments' pay policies
> effects of tax policies and inflation
> erosion of the divine right to manage
> change in company attitude to managers.

DEVELOPMENT

The good old days
  rise of the meritocracy
  the managerial revolution
  increase in management opportunities
  salary scales and increases compared with the cost
    of living
  differentials and fringe benefits
  summary: never had it so good!

Effects of pay policies
  under a Conservative government 1970–1974
    stage 1
    stage 2
    stage 3
  under a Labour government 1975 onwards
    removal of controls
    re-imposition of pay limits
  unequal effects on differentials of basic flat monetary
    increases and cut-off points at £5,000/£8,000
    for percentage increases.

Effects of tax policies and inflation
  government policies on redistribution of incomes

29

effect of income tax on higher incomes

reluctance to raise tax limits

failure of management salaries to keep up with cost of living comparisons with other countries

loss of differentials in conditions and fringe benefits by:

> new principles of taxation (Finance Act 1976)

extension to other groups (including shorter hours, flextime, longer holidays, pensions, loss of separate car parks and canteen facilities).

Erosion of 'the divine right to manage'

exercise of authority in a permissive society

power of shop stewards in non-management unions

growth of white-collar unionism among clerks and junior managers

legislation protecting employees (including race and sex discrimination, dismissal, trade union activities)

development of theories of behavioural science and industrial democracy.

Change in company attitude

rapid expansion, leading to loss of personal contact with directors

participation, leading to direct contact between main board and elected employee representatives and omission of managers from chain of communications

deteriorating market conditions, leading to closures of sites and loss of management jobs.

CONCLUSION

Summary of deterioration of managers' rewards since 1970, examination of the causes:

lack of organized strength to lobby government

fragmentation of power and influence

lack of knowledge about general economic and
social trends

lack of knowledge about practice within the
separate companies forming the group.

Demonstration that the services offered by the company-based union meet the real or imagined needs of individual managers.*

*(*Author's note:* The supporting evidence for this speech is fully set out in *Politics and Personnel Management: An outline history 1960–1976*, by Winifred Marks, Institute of Personnel Management 1978)

MEMORY AIDS

Once the framework is clear, superfluous material has been rejected and gaps filled, the speaker is ready to produce a draft of the full speech. This might take the form of an essay or extensive notes. From this draft he can develop the brief from which the speech will be made.

A few impressive speakers are able to make coherent, interesting speeches without so much as a note or a glance at their cuffs. The reasons for this are usually one or more of the following:

they are gifted speakers and have had considerable experience

they have reliable photographic memories

they have learned the framework by heart and practised the whole speech aloud until they are confident of their material, delivery and timing

they have given this speech or one almost identical to it on one or more previous occasions.

Inexperienced speakers without unusual gifts are advised to use memory aids. Learning the whole speech by heart is not recommended. Apart from the mental strain imposed on most speakers, spontaneity suffers and there is no chance to adjust to the mood of the audience. This ruse can also be detected at times by the speaker's appearance of looking into his own mind to find the words rather than communicating directly with the audience. Strain may also be apparent in his voice, which tends to become stilted and unnatural.

There is no golden rule about the use of notes. Spontaneity and speed of reaction to the audience are undoubtedly improved by having as few notes as possible and using the words that spring to mind as you go along. But this is of little use if the note is so brief that it fails to remind you of an important point or if stage-fright drives everything from your mind. You can be left wondering how to talk for five minutes on Egyptian mythology and whoever were Thoth, Horus and Anubis.

Reading a speech

Some speakers have their speeches typed out in full and read them word for word. This is advisable when giving an important lecture to members of a learned society in which every word is under scrutiny. It may be essential when the primary concern is that different audiences should have identical information, eg if the speech contains some matters of vital concern to an organization (a move to another site and arrangements for transfer), the chairman has already put out a statement for publication and the directors are passing on the message to different groups simultaneously.

These are extreme cases and the second hardly qualifies as a speech of the kind considered here.

Most speakers who read their speeches in full do so because they are afraid they will dry up in mid-sentence. This rarely occurs but it is better to guard against it, if you are of a worrying disposition, than to lie awake the whole night before imagining the worst.

If you must read your speech for whatever reason, make it appear as spontaneous as possible. The worst delivery is achieved by reading with head undeviatingly bent in the monotone small children adopt for reading in class.

Do not read a word at a time. Have the script clearly typed in double spacing with bold headings. If you wear spectacles, be sure to have the right ones for the distance. Then glance at the script, memorize the next few phrases and look at the audience while you are speaking. Everyone prefers to be looked at when being addressed. Apart from establishing a better personal relationship with the listeners, you will be able to adjust your performance to suit them, for instance by speaking more slowly or more clearly or repeating points, when you can see they are finding difficulty in following.

Television announcers are adept at this type of reading aloud, without even the incentive of being able to see their audience. With practice it can become impossible to tell whether the speech is being delivered from notes or read.

If you are reading because you are nervous, try not to advertize your nervousness. Speeches typed on large sheets of paper are floppy to hold and quickly give away a trembling hand. Make sure there is a lectern of the right height or take a stiff folder to support the papers.

Speaking from notes

At the opposite extreme to the verbatim readers are those who manage to compress their memory aids on to a few small cards. They usually have separate

cards for the introduction, every sub-section and the conclusion. The amount of information recorded on them reflects the speaker's self-confidence, breadth of knowledge and skill at recalling the facts, supporting evidence and anecdotes. Small cards are unobtrusive, easily handled and can even be waved about without causing too much distraction. In short, they are ideal for speakers with the necessary attributes.

Many speakers prefer fairly full notes, for example:

Egyptian mythology
> Thoth—god of the moon; patron of writing, learning, sciences; depicted as an ibis or a dog-faced baboon; tongue and will
> Horus—celestial and solar god; depicted as a falcon; enemy of Seth; heart and intellect
> Anubis—early god of the dead; depicted as a jackal

and so on.

This method has the advantage of reminding the speaker of all the points to be made without dictating the way in which they are put over. It means that you must know your subject thoroughly and this in itself gives confidence.

If you would prefer to use short notes but are unsure about your ability to cope with them, it is safer to adopt a belt-and-braces approach. Have your speech typed in full or in full note form and take with it the brief notes on cards. The reassurance of having the longer version will probably do away with the need to use it. But remember that if you do need it, you will want it in a hurry and possibly a panic. Have it clearly marked with headings and numbers corresponding to your place on the cards.

Starting to speak

Another safety precaution is to write down and memorize the first few sentences. Breaking the ice can prove difficult and the way in which a speech starts has a considerable effect on its reception.

If you have been introduced by the chairman of the meeting, you will first wish briefly to acknowledge his remarks. Only startling errors of fact should be corrected, eg 'It is true that I had some modest success with *The Messiah* but the credit for *Dido and Aeneas* must go to Purcell.' Any disclaimer of praise tends to sound like false modesty.

You may wish to add a few introductory remarks of your own. These should not take the form of an apology. The only exception is when some unavoidable reason has caused you to be late despite all precautions.

Never make excuses for your lack of material or preparation. If you had insufficient time to gather all the information you would have liked or to study it in depth, keep quiet about it and do your best with what you have. To disclose, for instance, that you have written the speech in the train on the way to the meeting is a slight to the audience and the chairman. It does nothing to enhance their opinion of the speaker. Refrain also from telling your listeners in advance that the subject matter is boring or you do not know how to present it in an interesting way. This will predispose them to find it uninteresting. If it is, they will find out soon enough.

Do not make apologies either, for your inexperience as a speaker. 'Unaccustomed as I am to public speaking' has become too hackneyed even to be used in jest, except by the most sophisticated.

Let your interest and enthusiasm be apparent from the start. It is better to be starry-eyed than boring.

Visual aids as memory aids

If you have decided to use visual aids prepared before-hand, these can be used as memory aids with or without notes. It is quite possible, for example, to talk entirely to a set of slides showing flora and fauna in the same patch of woodland through the four seasons to a group of naturalists or of an office block and the different types of work going on inside it at a careers convention.

Instead of the main points being written on cards, they can be photographed on slides or written on a flip chart, (*see* the chapter on Visual Aids page 68).

TIMING THE SPEECH

How much time is there?
From the original invitation you should know how
much time has been allowed for your speech. You
may have received a letter denoting half an hour's
talk or programmes with entries such as:

 9 00 Antisocial behaviour   I M Wright
10 30 Coffee
or
 9 00 Worker directors—a management and a trade
union view   Clive Scanlon
                                  Ivor Wright
10 30 Coffee

In all these cases you need more specific information.

Are you expected to talk for half an hour in the first
instance and then answer questions? If so, for how
long? Will the questioners confine themselves to the
subject matter of your speech or will they expect you
to cover related topics?

In the first programme, does the chairman's introduction start at or before 9 00? How long will it last? If
it is the first session of a course, he may well wish to

make generally welcoming remarks to the participants. It is not unknown for the aims of the whole conference to be expressed in detail before the first speaker is introduced. Try to forestall the loss of possibly half your time by having a time for the general introduction inserted in the programme or (if you saw it for the first time after printing) at least agreed beforehand.

An additional hazard is obvious in the second programme. How is the time to be shared between the two speakers? Are you to speak for half an hour each with half an hour for questions? If questions come thick and fast, is the coffee break likely to be postponed?

You need to know the exact time allowed for your speech so that you can decide:

> how much basic information can be packed into it
> how much secondary information and illustrative material
> which aids to use
> the manner of presentation.

The length of the speech should never exceed the length of time the audience can concentrate. As a rough guide, the more intelligent the audience, the more interested in and knowledgeable of the subject and the more used it is to absorbing information by ear for uninterrupted periods, the longer the speech can afford to be. A group of recently graduated nuclear physicists listening to a speech on how to control atomic radiation when the reactor is expected to explode will pay attention for a solid hour (provided the explosion does not actually occur during that time). Groups whose schooldays are far behind them and whose lives have been physically active rather

than contemplative are unlikely to concentrate loosely
on what is said for more than 30 minutes or concentrate
hard for half that time. The sound of elderly listeners
switching off deaf aids in order to slumber undisturbed
can be off-putting to a sensitive speaker. If in doubt
about the length of time for which you should speak,
err on the side of brevity.

The span of attention can obviously be increased
by the use of appropriate techniques, (*see* part II
beginning page 47). Variety is essential and, if possible,
participation by the audience. If your speech cannot
be compressed within the optimum listening time, it
helps to treat the main sections separately and to
sum up regularly. Questions may be taken at the end
of every section, as long as they are controlled so that
they do not cause any important points of the main
speech to be omitted, (*see: How to deal with questions* on
page 79).

Once you are sure of the times, stick closely to
them. Starting on time will please the audience and
help to put you in the right mood.

40

Finish on time as well. If you are taking part in a day's programme, a late finish will either deprive the audience of part of a necessary break or force a late start on all subsequent speakers. If you are the last or only speaker, you may be preventing some people from being punctual for their next appointment. If the speech is in the evening, the audience will be counting on going home to watch their favourite television serial or getting some refreshment before closing time or simply waiting to go to bed. Their goodwill will evaporate minute by precious minute.

Fitting the speech into the time
There is only one foolproof way of ensuring that your speech will take the allotted time, no more and no less. Try it out loud on a loved one (if prepared to listen without mocking) or even alone, preferably on a tape recorder. Time the spoken speech carefully and adjust the content as necessary, allowing a few minutes extra for the live performance since you will probably talk a little more slowly to a full audience than to one person or a towel rail.

For inexperienced speakers, an oral practice has the added benefit of accustoming them to the sound of their own solitary voices. One of the startling features of one's first formal speech is to hear the opening sentences travelling into space without any of the usual concomitants of conversation. There are no replies, no attempts to butt in, no grunts of approval or disapproval, only restrained body gestures in the typically well-behaved audience. This phenomenon becomes less strange with experience. Using the speech for oral practice has the advantage of making the content familiar but its use is not essential especially if the speech is still in preparation. Seize any opportunity of speaking, to the back of an empty hall or to an unattended flock of sheep. It is worth feeling silly on your own to overcome nervousness on the day. Do not be alarmed if your voice sounds strained, hard and unnatural in your own ears. Speaking with fervour in an empty barracks or to unheeding livestock is not a natural occupation. Simply having a genuine audience (as opposed to one or two conscripted and possibly uninterested loved ones) does wonders for those striving to communicate with it, from Sir John Gielgud to a raw speaker. The reality of the occasion and direct contact induce a more natural and warmer tone.

Over-rehearsal is a rare problem. Its possible disadvantages are that the speaker might become bored with his speech or hyper-critical of it. Dissatisfaction can be remedied by further work on the content or methods of presentation. Boredom vanishes before a live audience. Even a series of audiences hearing the same talk prevents boredom, as everyone reacts differently.

Time every section aloud as well as the whole speech. For an hour's talk the schedule might be:

9 30 introduction to main theme: adjustment to retirement
9 40 finance—how to plan ahead and manage on less income
9 55 physical health—diet and exercise
10 10 mental health—intellectual and social occupation
10 20 summary and conclusion.

It is helpful to include a few additional notes at the

end of every section about something which would interest the audience but is not essential to the development of the main theme. If you are ahead of time it can be used. If you are short of time it can be omitted and may still come in useful at question time.

Obviously you will need to keep any eye on the clock. The best place for it is at the back of the room above the audience's head. Failing this, take off your wrist watch and put it on the lectern or table where you can easily see it when glancing at your notes. This is less distracting than trying surreptitiously to slide back your cuff. Avoid the temptation of checking the time every few minutes. Practice will enable you to judge when 10 or 15 minutes have elapsed.

If you are amazed at how time has run on since you last checked, conceal your pleasure or panic and adjust the length of the rest of the speech. No one but yourself will be aware of your discomfiture unless you make it plain.

Part II
HOW TO HOLD THE ATTENTION OF THE AUDIENCE

INTRODUCTION

A speech is worthless unless the audience listens to it. Also the speaker has only one chance to gain and keep his hearers' attention. If he does not succeed, they are most unlikely to return to hear the same speech a second time. The content of the speech is, of course, of prime importance. People pay great attention to matters which in their opinion closely affect their personal welfare. A description of a current Martian invasion of the Outer Hebrides or an infallible roulette system would have everyone on the edge of the seat.

Most speeches are not of such vital concern as to ensure unflagging, strenuous efforts to hear and understand the content. It is the task of the speaker to present his case in a way which makes it easy to follow and to comprehend. It is more likely to be well received if he is personally acceptable or at least not irritating to his audience. He should choose the best words for the audience and use them in ways which not only clarify the meaning but make listening a pleasure.

Variety in presentation, emotional appeal and

humour, the use of visual and aural aids help to maintain and revive interest.

The physical comfort of the audience is the most mundane consideration but nevertheless important.

No one can be expected to give whole-hearted attention to a speech when he is gasping for fresh air, trying to alleviate backache, wriggling his toes in an attempt to stave off frostbite or not near enough to see.

PERSONAL STYLE

How to win friends
We all listen with more attention and with more
pleasure to someone we like and with whom we feel
at ease. We react instinctively against anyone who is
overbearing or aggressive or whom we suspect of
presenting a false front.

Be honest and forthright in your approach. Treat
the audience with consideration and on equal terms
and you will be well received.

You cannot always hope to have a message to
convey which will please the audience. It may be that
you have to make a speech with the aim of putting
right some procedure or practice which has been
wrongly or inefficiently carried out. This can be
achieved without carping criticism if you concentrate
on the defect, the reasons why it is causing inefficiency/
chaos/dismay and the practical measures needed to
put it right. By concentrating on the sin and not on
the sinner you avoid allocating blame, prevent the
adoption of defensive attitudes and substitute positive
remedial action.

Be natural
Only the smuggest are entirely satisfied with themselves but the place to practise a different personality
is not on a public speaking platform. Do not attempt
to put on an act. If you pretend, possibly for the sake
of the audience, to be more erudite, more sophisticated,
more important than you are, or if you strive to get
down to the audience's level (as you assess it) by
pretending to know less than you do or talking with
an assumed accent, you will appear a sham. A speaker
meets his audience on equal human terms. Both need
to accept and trust the other in order to derive the
greatest benefit from the speech.

For the same reasons, do not try to suppress your
personality. Use your normal expressions of speech
in your talk (always provided they are suitable for
mixed company) rather than strive for a flawless
prose style. If your emotions are aroused by certain
aspects of your case, do not be ashamed to show it.
People identify more readily with one martyr than a
host of abstract ideals.

Relax
Public speaking is not intended to be a relaxing
experience. The slight anxiety engendered should
improve performance not stultify it. The best antidote
to excessive nervousness is to arrive in good time with
a well-prepared speech.

After you have checked the physical arrangements
and decided where you will stand and put your notes,
try to put the speech out of your mind. Chat to the
chairman or any of the audience who may be about
on some neutral topic. If no one is available go for a
walk around the building, do a crossword or practise

deep breathing. It is relaxing simply to take several long, deep breaths, filling the base of the lungs and activating the diaphragm. More sophisticated techniques have been advocated, such as holding the nose between thumb and middle finger, with the index finger on the bridge and pressing the nostrils in turn to enforce breathing through each one alternately. This is at least distracting.

Before going on to the platform or place where the speech is to be given, act calmly and you will feel calmer. Move and talk more slowly than usual. Let your muscles relax consciously, especially across the shoulders and at the back of the neck. However little you feel like it, make a conscious effort to smile preferably when entirely alone or, if constantly attended, at the mild pleasantries of your companion. This removes all traces of an anxious frown or pout and helps to relax facial muscles before you face the audience. Constant smiling when speaking, however, can make the speaker appear patronizing or insufficiently aware of the gravity of his subject or over-anxious to the point of trying to curry favour or simply below par. Relax beforehand and your facial expressions will adjust naturally to the reactions of the audience.

It can be a mistake to try to induce Dutch courage by taking alcohol or drugs of any kind, especially if you are not accustomed to them. Remember Kingsley Amis's Lucky Jim! It is better to suffer a little nervousness than to run the risk of being unaware of what you are saying.

Personal presentation

Dress
You will feel more relaxed when speaking if you are

comfortably and appropriately dressed. Clothes, hairstyles, accessories and make-up should be suitable for the particular occasion. Full evening dress (with medals) would be as unsuitable for an informal talk to the village youth club as denims and leather boots at a formal dinner.

The only general guidance which can be offered is that clothes should not be restricting, particularly so tight as to make deep breathing difficult and should be free from loose ends and trimmings conducive to fiddling. If you stand to speak, comfortable shoes are an asset, even if your new high heels are more fashionable. For every individual the boundary between the need for comfort and the confidence engendered by looking as smart as possible will be drawn in a different place. The speaker's appearance should not be so outrageous as to alienate the audience nor so outlandish as to be distracting.

Speakers of both sexes should check over their dress before appearing in public, to ensure that all vital buttons and fastenings are secure and that nothing is in danger of working loose or falling off in the excitement of speaking. Nothing rivets the gaze like a slowly unfastening zip but attention is diverted from the speech.

Women speakers can avoid the necessity of sitting for long periods with knees together by asking for a modesty board or a long baize cloth for the table. This also allows men to twist their legs into convoluted shapes unobserved.

Stance
There is no law of nature that says a speech must be delivered standing up. The advantage of standing is

that the speaker has a better view of the audience and vice versa. If your knees are weak from exertion, nervousness or rheumatism, it is perfectly permissible to speak sitting down.

If you stand, there is a temptation to walk about. This should be resisted. Stand in an easy, relaxed position in one place and move only for a purpose, such as writing on a board or pointing to a line on a chart. On no account wander among the audience, even if it is seated in a U shape. Inevitably you will present your back to part of it and make listening difficult.

It would be unnatural not to move your hands at all but there is no need to emulate Magnus Pyke. They can hold notes, be clasped behind your back, even occasionally hidden in pockets (provided there are no coins there to rattle). They should not toss up and catch pieces of chalk or describe wild parabolas with felt pens or fiddle with clothing or scratch or point accusing fingers. Above all they must not tap or caress the microphone; ear-splitting noises result.

If you are aware of any irritating habits, such as wagging your beard, putting your spectacles on and off, swinging your pearls or standing on the sides of your shoes, try to abstain from them while speaking. Any opportunity of recording all or part of your speech on closed circuit television should be snapped up. It brings to light expressions and mannerisms speakers never knew they possessed.

In short, in delivery, dress, deportment and behaviour, there should be nothing which distracts attention away from what the speaker is saying.

HOW TO CHOOSE AND USE
THE RIGHT WORDS

Clarity and simplicity

Treating the audience as equals does not mean
addressing it in terms only the speaker can understand.
On the contrary, respect for the other person will
ensure that you put forward your ideas in language
he will understand without effort.

Speech is less easy to follow than the printed word.
If a sentence or a phrase is unclear when read, the
reader can re-read it. If he meets a word he does not
understand, he can look it up in a dictionary. In a
speech there is no opportunity to ask for enlightenment
at the time of utterance and what has been misunderstood is difficult to recall at question time.

It is doubly important, therefore, to speak in simple
clear terms and to use short sentences. Eschew subordinate clauses, especially between the subject and
verb or verb and object. The following sentence is
well nigh impossible to follow verbally and should be
rephrased as at least three separate sentences:

As the city-state, although it was the classical

Greek political unit, an autonomous community idealized as the highest form of human association, resulted in disunity, the collapse of the Greek polity was inevitable.

Paragraphs in the speech should also be kept short ie a single idea should be expressed in a few simple sentences. The simplicity of explanation and the amount of repetition will be determined by the capacity of the audience to absorb information.

The attention of the audience is attracted by matters of concern to itself, not by generalizations. Abstract ideas appeal mainly to abstract philosophers. Ordinary listeners follow more easily concrete terms. The implications are clear: avoid impersonal constructions and illustrate your ideas with concrete words and imagery.

'I believe' or 'Doctor Strabismus believes' is better than 'It is believed'. 'Plants need light and water' is better than 'It is generally accepted that plants need light and water.'

When Sir Winston Churchill wanted to convey the idea that safeguarding the nation's future by ensuring proper feeding of the next generation was of great importance, he said 'There is no finer investment for any community than putting milk into babies.' (Radio broadcast 21 March 1943).

The scramble for power within institutions and its deleterious effect upon character is succinctly portrayed by the simple phrase 'the rat race'.

The words you use will be determined by the level of understanding of your subject among the least knowledgeable of your audience. If you are giving a talk on the application of advanced statistical methods, you might safely assume that you could talk about percentages without fear of misunderstanding. If you regularly show labour turnover charts to a monthly meeting of the works committee, it would be wise to ensure that percentages are included in training courses for newly promoted managers and newly elected employee representatives.

If your audience is a cross-section of the community at large, some of them will not know what a percentage is. In that case do not use the mysterious word. To say '65 per cent were rejected' and then go on to explain what a percentage is, savours of patronising. Simply say '65 out of every 100' or '650 out of 1000' and no one is made to feel ignorant.

It is the mark of an expert to be able to make technical matters readily comprehensible to laymen. Anyone who doubts whether this is possible should watch Blue Peter when a knotty technical operation is being described to children.

Any technical term likely to be unfamiliar to some of the audience should be explained the first time it occurs. Not everyone appreciates the significance of habeas corpus or half-life. Organizations and Acts of Parliament should be given their full titles, not referred to by initials eg the World Health Organization, the Commission on Industrial Relations, the Royal National Lifeboat Institution, the Church Missionary Society, the National Cyclists' Union. This at least serves to avoid confusion between the Industrial Relations Act and the Irish Republican Army.

If initials must be used or are likely to be used unthinkingly after the first few minutes, write out the titles in full for the audience and put them where people can refer to them during the speech. This might be on a wall chart or on handouts placed on seats.

If you are uncertain whether the audience will understand a certain technical term, it is tactful to give the explanation first and then the term: 'The plain rectangular block on which the statue stands, the socle, has been eroded.'

Jargon should be treated with the same reserve before a non-professional audience as swear words, ie left out altogether. As H W Fowler points out in his *Dictionary of Modern English Usage* a 'relatively unstructured conversational interaction' is better described as an 'informal talk'.

Beware particularly of words which have a common meaning and a specialized one. A simple word like 'boned' means quite the opposite to a fishmonger and a corsetier. If such words are used, the exact meaning should be defined.

Plain, short, Anglo-Saxon words are more easily heard and understood than long, fanciful derivations from Greek and Latin. Formal words have their place in some professions, notably the law, from the policeman who proceeds to the scene of the crime instead of just going there, to the advocate's peroration (summing up). For most writers and practically all speakers it is more effective to use:

    rooms rather than accommodation
    buy rather than purchase
    send rather than transmit
    foresee rather than visualize
    begin rather than commence

and so on and on.

Slang should be used sparingly. Unless you are

57

aware of the latest fashionable words, your speech will sound dated. A young audience tends to be particularly critical of an older speaker who uses slang, even where the age gap is of five years or less. His slang may quite accurately reflect the latest fashion but to the audience he may appear that embarrassing figure, a retarded adolescent. Already *with it* and *in* can no longer be used to express these sentiments. If your intention is to present yourself in a humorous light as a relic of the 1940s, however, *wizard prang* would be absolutely topping!

Other fashionable words, though not strictly speaking slang, should be avoided. They tend to be inserted with little regard for style or clarity. To a marketing manager every composite concept is a mix; to an industrial relations manager it is a package. Not long ago everything was *-wise* eg fashionwise, moneywise, workwise, with little regard to wisdom. Now everything finds itself *in a situation:* in the school situation (in schools), in the home situation (at home), in a labour surplus situation (when jobs are scarce) or *involved* in any number of predicaments.

Unnecessary words should be left out. This particularly applies to space fillers such as *you know, I mean, um* and *er*. Listen to yourself and other people having an ordinary conversation and you will be amazed at the number of times these occur. Better still, have a tape recording of an impromptu conversation typed back word for word. The offending words are even more striking in print.

Flowery language also hampers the flow of thought and distracts attention from the message. Paradoxically superlatives weaken rather than strengthen the whole speech. If they are sprinkled generously around, they become commonplace and lose their value. Any word not qualified is weakened. Attempts to repair the damage by doubling superlatives then compounds the problem.

A beautiful sunset is more lovely than *a very, very beautiful sunset. I heard Jim singing* is more convincing than *I am absolutely sure I heard Jim singing.*

Unless you are speaking to the French Club or the German Expatriate Society foreign words are sure to confuse some of the audience. Use the nearest English equivalent. Most sentiments can be appreciated equally well in English, even the maxims of La Rochefoucauld. 'Nous avons tous assez de force pour supporter les maux d'autrui' is just as good when rendered 'We all have enough strength to bear the misfortunes of others' and will be understood by everyone.

If the point relies entirely on word play in the original language it will either not be appreciated or take so much explanation that the subtlety will be lost.

The unnecessary use of long words, abstruse professional and technical terms, leads audiences to believe that the speaker is more concerned to display his erudition than to communicate effectively with them.

Short, simple, concrete words in short sentences and paragraphs are the best vehicles to express well thought out ideas.

It is easy and useful to test your speech for comprehensibility before hand. If it is typed in full, ask your typist not to type it mechanically but to read it and let you know if there is anything in it she cannot understand. Or else ask the same service of the long suffering loved one on whom you try out the speech verbally. Any comments must be accepted in a spirit of humble gratitude and acted upon or your speech will not benefit and next time you will be assured that all is crystal clear.

Pronunciation

There is no point in giving a speech which is inaudible. However excellent the content, however masterly the choice of words, all is wasted if the audience simply cannot hear what you say.

You are not expected to shout. If the room or hall is too large or the acoustics too muffled to enable you to be heard by the back row when speaking clearly, you should have a microphone. Usually this is not necessary.

There are several ways in which clarity of speech can be improved instantly:

by taking deep breaths before starting and whenever possible during the speech, certainly at the end of every paragraph

by looking at the audience and speaking directly to different members of it (not transfixing one). Try to avoid concentrating on the first few rows and shift your eyes from face to face. This has the added benefit of focussing the audience's attention on you. Listeners are less likely to go into a brown study or further if they think you will see them being so impolite

by speaking more slowly than usual and pausing before important words. This should not mean deteriorating into a drawl or becoming so slow that the audience loses the thread. The pace should be varied to maintain interest. A short pause after an important statement or before a vital word helps to emphasize it

by enunciating consonants clearly. It is consonants rather than vowels which distinguish one word from another. Without vowels the last sentence could still be read: t s cnsnnts rthr thn vwls whch dstngsh n wrd frm nthr. Without consonants it would be impossible. A whisper can be clearly heard if the consonants are crisp

by pronouncing every word separately. Names are often difficult to hear correctly unless the words are separated. Many a Miss de Whatever has been expected as Mr Whatever

by pitching your voice a shade higher if it is normally low. But remember, that nervousness often causes the voice to rise anyway

by varying your intonation as you would if you were reading a play and taking all the parts yourself. The emotional tone may range from icy cold to warm and slushy.

If you use a microphone, you may find that it distorts the sound a little, often by making Ss hiss. This letter is impossible to omit but it can be kept short. The microphone may also give an echo which you can hear. Your inclination is then to wait until you have finished speaking in the echo before going on to the next sentence. Do not worry about this unless the time lag is large. It will slow down your speech only a little and aid comprehension.

Again, if you use a microphone test it before the audience arrives to make sure it is working as well as testing it for echoes. Get someone else to speak into it while you stand at the front, back and middle of the hall to experience how the audience will hear. If the noise is overpowering, get the volume turned down or do without the microphone altogether. Before taking this step it is as well to make sure that you can be heard in the back row.

Accents
Regional accents are in fashion and can be endearing. A talk on the hard life of a cottage chainmaker is much enhanced by an authentic Black Country accent. For broadcasting gardeners an accent is almost a necessity. There is no need to strive for standard English pronunciation (whatever that may be). The only proviso is that those whose accents are so pronounced as to make them incomprehensible outside a radius of 10 miles from their birthplace should confine their speaking engagements within that area. Even in these cases, clarity can often be achieved by excluding dialect words. *Zummat* may be imperfectly understood where *Zomething* is clear.

Misunderstandings which arise can sometimes be detected from the mystification reflected in the faces of the audience. The headmistress who was heard to say at a parents' meeting 'I want the children to take pot in the classroom, to take pot in games, to take pot in social activities' quickly amended her rendering of *part*.

Careful phrasing also helps. A Lancastrian collecting his suitcase from a left luggage office in London was amazed to be told 'You left a pie on this'. A different arrangement of syllables clarified the meaning: 'You'll have to pay on this'.

It is essential to remember to speak slowly and

distinctly, to vary pace and intonation and to keep a watchful eye on the audience.

Emotional appeal

Audiences listen more attentively and respond more sympathetically if their emotions are aroused. There are many ways of setting about this, some on an instinctive level.

You can induce pleasant feelings in the audience by praising the achievements of the group to which its members belong or admiring its courage in the face of adversity. Needless to say, the tributes must be specific and must be sincere if they are to be effective, eg 'It is a pleasure to speak to singers whose rendering of *Pineapple Poll* was so enthusiastic. The costumes and scenery were a triumph of invention and sheer hard work, considering the short time at your disposal between the fire and the first performance.' Or you can speak in an appreciative way of a subject known to be dear to the audience's heart, from the song of the nightingale to the Tolpuddle martyrs. The use of humour also helps. If you can amuse people, they are disposed to like you and will tolerate some of your shortcomings.

Emotional involvement is achieved by illustrating points with incidents taken from life, so that the audience can identify with the characters in the case histories and share their joy or distress. It is easier to absorb information about the problems of battered wives if they are related to the actual experiences of Mrs Smith, forced to leave home with multiple injuries, and her search for shelter for her two babies.

Much less promising material can be treated in this way. The talk about management trade unionism (above) followed the fortunes of Alan, who started as a hopeful science graduate in 1963, a cheerful bachelor of 22 living with his parents in style on a salary of £1500, joining in the old Staff Association's cricket matches and cheese and wine parties. By 1973 he was shown to have acquired a large mortgage and 17 dependants (a widowed mother, a wife, four children, two hamsters, a gerbil, a cat, a pedigree Labrador and six pups) and was finding it difficult to manage on £6000. By 1978 they were all presumed to be sharing the last tin of Pedigree Chum (in fact they had started to rear chickens and were producing all their eggs and some of their meat).

A good speaker can arouse storms of indignation and/or enthusiasm. If the intention is to turn this to practical use, outlets should be made available on the spot. It may not be possible to rush off from the meeting and storm the barricades but the audience can be invited to sign a roster of duties for clearing overgrown footpaths or issued with a checklist of questions for the new goods inward procedure. At worst a box by the exit for the cause enables some of the goodwill to be tangibly expressed.

Humour

One of the surest ways of getting and holding the attention of the audience is by using humour. When members of the audience want to hear a comedian, however, they are better advised to stay at home and watch television; they often do. If they turn up to hear a speech, they want the speaker to concentrate on the subject at issue. The humour should arise from the subject matter. Jokes and funny anecdotes should simply illuminate the points the speaker is trying to make.

Practically no subject is so serious or so distressing that it has no humorous aspect. A general knowledge test (long since abandoned) for office applicants posed the question: 'With what sport do you associate the Ashes?' The answer was once given as '*Cremation*'. A report of an Industrial Tribunal in 1978 contained the following dictum: 'A person's employment is terminated by suicide; a resignation is superfluous.'

Humorous material abounds, for most talks, on library shelves, in magazines and newspapers and on the wireless and television. If your talk is on a topical subject, it could be worth reading *Punch* to see how it strikes other people. The point that the number of able managers emigrating because of working conditions in the UK had increased from 100 a week in 1977 to 200 a week in 1978 was aptly illustrated by the title of a current BBC programme: 'Will the last businessman to leave the country please put out the light?''

A sense of humour is an individual characteristic. Material gathered from external sources should be carefully blended into the framework of the speech, not in order to be disguised as original but to avoid distracting changes in presentation and style.

The best material comes from the speaker's own experience. It is then original and apposite. Anyone liable to be asked to speak regularly would do well to compile a folder of funny experiences. These can be quite simple, like typing errors ('Participation ensures that every employee is able to play a part in ruining the business') or remarks overheard in bus queues ('Those are nice shoes. Are they Hush Puppies?' 'No, they're Barker's').

This material also carries conviction. A fisherman describing the one that got away by pulling him into the river can be hilarious; the same story told by a third party is more likely to raise a thin smile.

Be objectively critical of your own jokes. A remark which sounded witty at the time may lose its point in retrospect without a great deal of supporting and tedious narrative.

Humour in a speech should always be kindly. It is easy to raise a cheap laugh at the expense of an individual or a group known to be unpopular with the audience. This is not only discourteous but will embarrass some listeners because their best friends are vegetarians or cyclists, or militant shop stewards or all three.

Blue jokes, however relevant, should be reserved for the Rugby Club's stag dinner. You may inadvertently use an expression with a double meaning which strikes you only as you utter it. Do not draw attention to the gaffe by explaining, for instance, that you meant the learned barrister had been a solicitor, not that he had earned his living by soliciting. It is better to go straight on without quivering an eyelid and hope that the few who noticed will soon forget.

The edge of a good joke is blunted by leading into it with 'I must tell you something funny' or 'One of my favourite funny stories'. Audiences resent the implication that they are unable to see a joke without forewarning or to judge for themselves whether it is amusing.

If you embark on a funny story, be sure to finish it. It is exasperating to become interested just as the speaker goes off at a tangent and never gets back to the point. For similar reasons a funny story should be short. One that rambles on and on not only ceases to be amusing but takes time which a well-planned speech cannot afford to lose.

Some speakers throw away really funny lines with a dead-pan expression. If the audience is quick to grasp allusions, this can be highly effective. A smile at one's own witticism is more usual. Laughter is not recommended. You may be the only one laughing.

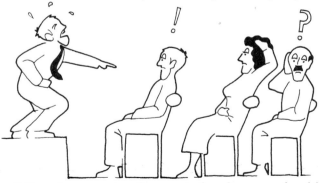

Like other aspects of presentation, humour should not be artificial or strained. Use your natural style.

VISUAL AIDS

The function of visual aids is to help the audience to appreciate a point more readily and to reinforce the spoken word. They can also help the speaker by taking the place of written notes in full or in part. They may be complex or simple but in every case they must be clearly seen or they entirely lose their point. Prepare them on the assumption that some members of the audience will be short-sighted, will come without their spectacles and will sit near the back.

Visual aids are useful in all but the most formal lectures. Most people absorb information more easily through their eyes than their ears. Television increases this tendency. Even having a speaker to watch focuses the attention better than simply hearing a speech, as on the wireless. Visual aids reinforce this reaction by creating diversions and adding variety. Different types may be used if appropriate during one speech.

Blackboards
The blackboard is an old schoolroom favourite and still found in many training departments. It is useful

for making points as the speech progresses. It can be used to build up a theory point by point, eg by drawing Maslow's ladder and filling in the rungs while expounding the theory of a hierarchy of needs.

It can also be used for jotting down points made by the audience in discussion time. Writing can be easily erased thus giving unlimited writing space, that is if a rubber is available. This should be checked, as well as the supply of chalk in the right colours.

Writing on the board needs practice if it is to be clearly legible. Frequent rubbing out makes this more difficult as the background becomes messy. The amount of time spent with your back to the audience needs to be kept to a minimum and broken up by turning and addressing it. Speaking to the blackboard is unproductive.

Charts

These advantages are preserved and the disadvantages lessened by substituting large sheets of plain paper or flip charts and felt pens for blackboard and chalk. The added advantages are that some material can be prepared to a high standard of presentation before-hand and saved for another occasion if needed. Clear writing is easier and colours more vivid.

Paper is expensive but easier to carry about even than cardboard charts. Before setting off with a roll under your arm, you should make sure that a suitable stand is available in the lecture room as a support. A blackboard and easel and two large bulldog clips are all that is required.

Stiff cardboard charts can be effectively prepared in advance using Letraset, coloured inks and professional services where justifiable. The justification is usually the need to use the same chart on many occasions, especially to show running totals like monthly sales or population trends.

Again you should check that you can display your chart without having to stand and hold it until your arms ache. The useful blackboard easel will double as a stand.

If you expect to carry stiff charts any distance, do not make them longer than the distance from armpit to knuckles.

Slides

There are times when one picture really is worth a thousand words and conveys the speaker's meaning far more accurately. It is much easier to show a slide of the new office block at Beccles than to describe in detail an eight storey building. Slides can be used to illustrate part of a talk or can form the basis around which the speech is built. They need not be confined to pictures but can incorporate headings, diagrams and legend. A talk to a careers convention of school-leavers might be based entirely on slides showing people at work in different occupations with close-ups of the machinery, products and records on which they are engaged, with shots of the canteen, social and sports club for light relief.

Slides are the smallest and lightest aids to carry about, can be delightful to look at and reduce the need for notes. But they are not without considerable disadvantages. They are shown in darkness, which prevents the speaker seeing the audience and so diminishes direct contact between them. Darkness, especially in a warm room, is conducive to sleep

70

despite the extra interest generated by the pictures. It also renders it impossible for the speaker to refer to notes unless there is a faint light over his lectern.

Slides must be prepared in advance and the photography of a high standard. Blurred slides or those in which there is so much detail that the main point is obscured are worse than useless. Good slides are often in demand by several speakers covering similar topics. If your organization has a pool of slides, be sure you have all those you need for your talk in the correct sequence.

Slides are small and light but if the screen and projector have to be provided by the speaker, they are heavy and cumbersome to transport and suitable electric fittings must be available in the lecture room. The projector has to have an operator. If this is the speaker, he may well be behind the audience and will have to brave the danger of slides appearing upside down and/or back to front. Automatic slide changers with remote control enable the speaker to face the audience but he should make sure that he understands the mechanism for moving on and recalling slides.

If an assistant is provided to operate the projector, a system of communications should be agreed and practised. In one university's main lecture theatre the speaker is on a stage and the operator in a projection room high above the balcony, reached by several flights of outside stairs. Communication is a matter of ringing an electric bell an agreed number of times. If the system is imperfectly understood or the speaker's finger slips, unexpected images appear, disappear and reappear in bewildering confusion.

An overhead projector can be useful if there is one available in the room but it would normally be much too cumbersome to transport. It has the advantage that the speaker can operate it himself in normal, shady daylight, facing the audience. As the material is prepared beforehand on special plates (or a continuous roll) a high standard of presentation is possible.

Films

A short film or videotape may be used as part of a speech to make a particular point and add variety. A film of the company chairman giving the annual results could precede a talk on the results of a particular department. Scenes from professional ballet and folk dance festivals would enhance a talk on the development of dancing.

Only professional films or amateur films of a high standard and stringently edited are likely to be acceptable to today's sophisticated audiences. Indiscriminate admiration of home movies has been lost by over-exposure to family holiday scenes.

A darkened room is necessary for films but videotapes can be viewed in normal daylight where closed circuit television facilities are available.

Summary

Visual aids should be used only when their contribution to the interest and understanding of the speech justifies the effort involved in their preparation and their use during the speech. If they are used, the speaker should be fully accustomed to using them and should ensure not only that the proper equipment and power points are available but that they are in proper working order on the night. He should also be thoroughly conversant with the material shown. A slide of the Doge's Palace appearing on the screen in the middle of a talk on British domestic architecture does not inspire confidence.

It is sometimes tempting to use visual aids conveniently developed and packaged by professionals. There may be some which are not only excellent but exactly what you need to illustrate your speech. Always take the precaution, however, of checking them thoroughly for yourself before incorporating them in the framework of the speech. Advertisements have been known to overstate the excellence of the product. Presentation of the originals is usually good but the standard of copies may have deteriorated, especially of films on frequent loan.

Material which is precisely relevant to the needs of a specific talk to a particular audience is hard to find. Inappropriate material is worse than useless.

The advantages of time-saving, standard of presentation and relevance should be carefully assessed when deciding whether to prepare your own visual aids, buy or borrow them from professional dealers or speak without them.

THE PHYSICAL COMFORT OF THE AUDIENCE

The physical conditions in which they listen will affect the amount of attention members of the audience will be able to devote to the speech. In ideal conditions they will not be aware of their surroundings yet remain wide awake.

Seating

Chairs should be upright with support for the arms, if possible, but not for the head. They should comfortably accommodate large men without making the feet of small women dangle in mid-air. Chairs with wide seats and short legs will achieve this and prevent anyone's blood supply being cut off at the thighs. There should be no sharp ridges to bite into the backs of knees or to inflict torture under the shoulder blades. On the other hand, padded armchairs will inevitably encourage some to go to sleep.

It is not as obvious as it sounds to say that all seats should face the speaker. Speakers are sometimes faced with problems such as giving an after-dinner speech from the centre of a long, narrow dining hall:

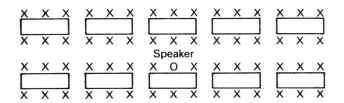

This is a physical impossibility. Whichever way the speaker faces, at least half the audience will be unable to hear. On one occasion when this happened, the room was so long that even if the speaker had stood at one end he could not have made himself heard at the other. In the event, the whole audience was moved to another room. The gain in audibility more than compensated for some loss of the after-dinner atmosphere.

If such drastic action is impossible in similar circumstances, the only alternative is for the audience to move its chairs into more rational positions. In less awkward situations the speaker can place himself more strategically.

Usually the seats are arranged facing the speaker in straight or curved rows. If the audience is small, seats may be placed in a U behind tables or even in a cosy semicircle.

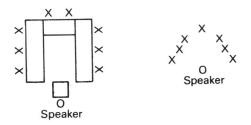

These arrangements contribute to a relaxed and informal atmosphere.

Sometimes the only room available is known to be far too large for the audience or a huge hall is booked and only a fraction of the expected numbers turn up. Bashfulness will cause people to keep out of the first rows but you need to insist that they sit together in the front. Having a few souls scattered in ones and twos over a large area ruins personal communication.

A few halls have fixed seating and a curtain which can be drawn part way across to isolate the front rows. In others the seats are movable. A space can then be created behind the minimum number of rows and if necessary accentuated by placing one row of chairs upside down on the first back row not to be used. Although this looks as if the cleaners are about to start work, it is effective and is not visible to the audience once it is seated. An even simpler remedy is to go provided with a few lengths of coloured tape to tie across the arms of the first of the unwanted back rows. If the front rows fill up and people continue to arrive, all that is necessary is to untie the tape.

A strong-minded usher can work wonders. If all else fails, tell the audience you want them in the front and do not start until they move. As a lecturer in the London School of Economics' large lecture hall put it: 'This is a theatre, ladies and gentlemen, not a cinema. The best seats are at the front.'

Noise

A high level of background noise strains the speaker's voice and the audience's ears. The ideal rooms are sound-proof but these are still rare and tend to have compensatory defects such as being underground.

The most one can hope for is that the room will be well away from:

busy roads

factory areas where, for example, machines are making tins and trucks delivering steel plates on concrete floors

receiving and despatch areas in shops, factories, offices and hotels, where lorries are unloading refrigerators, sugar by suction pumps, tons of stationery or barrels of beer

canteens and large kitchens, especially with machinery for washing large quantities of crockery and cutlery

the typing pool.

If the only room available is in one of these unenviable positions, try to choose a time when work has finished or goods are not being delivered. It may still be necessary to send an envoy to stop temporarily the removal of floorboards from the room above.

Temperature and ventilation

To keep the audience alert, the room should be slightly cooler than the temperature at which most people keep their centrally heated sitting rooms. The air should be fresh (not stale) but no one should be forced to sit in a draught.

Conflict often arises between the need for quiet and the need for fresh air. If windows are opened, noise or music pours in from the street, or comes from building repairs in neighbouring offices. Ventilation systems with fans for extracting used air can be almost as noisy. Some pipes and radiators clank loudly when expanding and contracting.

It is advisable to check the ventilation system beforehand. The room may be just the right temperature before the audience arrives but body heat will build up during the session, as medieval barons realized when they packed their castles with serfs before a reception.

It is increasingly common to find smoking forbidden in public places or at least prohibited in certain areas, such as parts of restaurants and the front seats in theatres, buses and aeroplanes. To minimize the risk of coughing during your speech for yourself and the nearest members of the audience you could ask for this facility if it is not already available for the front seating area.

If it is impossible to regulate the temperature and ventilation quietly and effectively during the speech, make sure the room is well aired beforehand and cooler than most people would prefer. They will then become more comfortable as the talk progresses, rather than more and more uncomfortably hot and sleepy. If the central heating system is going to punctuate a Mozart symphony like a faulty metronome, turn it off.

HOW TO DEAL WITH QUESTIONS

Purpose of questions

After most talks time is set aside for questions from the audience and general discussion. The length of time to be allowed should be agreed with the chairman of the meeting, whose duty it is to bring the proceedings to a halt at the correct time. The audience should be told whether there will be an opportunity to ask questions, so that members can make a mental or written note during the speech of any points not fully understood or about which they would like more information. If question time is not mentioned on the programme, the chairman may refer to it in opening the meeting. If all else fails, the speaker should make it clear that he will be delighted or at least prepared to answer questions after speaking.

Most speakers welcome questions as an opportunity to gauge the effect of their talk. Pertinent questions from different people designed to clarify a difficulty or to pursue an interesting point which the speaker has had time only briefly to mention indicate general understanding and usually appreciation.

Answering them is no problem to speakers who know their subject.

Questions which show a point has been misunderstood provide the chance to make a second, clearer statement and for the speaker to ask the audience questions until he is satisfied that everyone has grasped the point.

Breaking the ice

A complete silence when questions are invited may mean that:

> the talk has been absolutely lucid and comprehensive
>
> the audience is taking time to prepare thoughtful questions
>
> the audience has gone to sleep through at least part of it and is afraid to ask questions lest this fact be revealed
>
> it has been far above the listeners' heads and they are anxious not to appear ignorant.

As it is disquieting not to know which of these is the cause, some exchange of views should be provoked.

Always be prepared with more material than you intend to use in your speech. If you have a chairman or friends in the audience, they can usually be relied to ask the first question. They can even be primed to do so, if you are apprehensive.

Some audiences are shy about asking questions, especially if it means getting to their feet and confessing to their names. This practice is nevertheless encouraged after business speeches, when questioners are asked to state their names and the companies for which they work. The rest of the audience find it interesting to be able to relate the question to its context (eg large or small organization, commercial, industrial, civil service or professional) and the information certainly helps the speaker to answer more pertinently.

Give people a few minutes in which to screw up their courage but do not let the silence become so oppressive that no one dares to break it. In the interim elaborate one of the controversial topics in your speech in a chatty way, inviting anyone to interrupt who is moved to do so.

Asking an unresponsive audience questions serves to change the tone and style and may well provoke a response. It also entails some risk. You may have to answer them yourself. At least you can be prepared for your own questions and, as the comedians say, it is pleasant to enjoy an intelligent conversation now and then.

Another technique is to say something quite outrageous like 'Red meat is necessary for the full development of intelligence' to the Vegetarian Society. Then encourage the most vociferous objector to make a coherent statement.

Once the ice has been broken, several people will jump in.

Honest answers to honest questions

Give genuine answers to genuine questions. Do not be tempted to evade any issue. If you do not know the answer, do not try to cover up. Refer the questioner to the appropriate source of information. If the answer is necessary to him in order to carry out more effectively something you want done, offer to find out and send it to him. In this case be sure you know the enquirer's name and address and make a note so that you do not forget.

Some questioners have difficulty in framing their questions. In these cases, listen to what they are trying to say and answer the underlying query rather than the actual words. The question actually asked may be easier to answer but resist the temptation or you will not help the questioner. Some questions clearly show that the listener has missed the point. If the answer was given in the speech, it does no harm to explain it again simply and briefly without, of course, mentioning that it has been covered already. A short recapitulation serves to impress the argument upon other members of the audience. Irrelevant and impossibly difficult questions can be gently deflected by such gambits as 'That is an interesting observation. I do not know of any practical effects of drilling for North Sea oil on the migratory habits of reindeer but shall look out for references to it from now on.'

Always look for something to commend in the most extraordinary questions: 'I am afraid I cannot help with any statistics on mortality rates among sharks from yellow fever in Sumatra but your contention that alligators carry the disease merits further research.'

The word of encouragement should end the sentence. It is less pleasing to be told 'Your point on the use of charcoal as fuel for lorries was well made but the practical difficulties are likely to be insuperable', than 'Despite all the practical difficulties your point was well made'.

In other words, never belittle any questioner. Civility will not be misinterpreted as gullibility. Other members of the audience are capable of assessing the value of questions and will be encouraged by your method of dealing with the lunatic fringe to frame better questions of their own and ask them without fear.

Obviously you would never deliberately try to make anyone look foolish or ignorant before an audience. It is akin to reprimanding a subordinate in public. Members of the audience can also assess the value and underlying motives of questions.

Dealing with devious questions

Practically all questions are serious and helpful but in any audience there may be one or two who seek to use question time for their own selfish ends rather than genuine enlightenment.

There is the frustrated orator who thinks he should have given the talk in the first place and who attempts to restate the whole case at length with minor differences. Be ready to glide in with a brief comment as soon as he draws breath and pass quickly to the next questioner. The audience will approve. It came to hear you.

There is the saboteur who attends only to put forward his own view of the subject and closes his mind to any arguments you put forward. His question may be formed in this way:

> In view of the serious financial difficulties/shortage of space/staffing problems/lack of equipment facing the organization at this time, would you not agree that the measures you propose are impractical? Would it not be better to improve cash flow/move to Scotland/recruit more engineers/buy a computer?

Again intervene briefly before the audience is subjected to a second speech. If the point is relevant, you have probably covered it already and can recap the main arguments. If it is a red herring, you should decline to comment on the grounds of irrelevance. Do not be drawn into a long discussion on a totally different subject. That is not what the audience came to hear and its time will be wasted as well as yours.

Hecklers are rare. If you have one in the audience, do not allow yourself to become angry. At least do not betray anger. A heated exchange quickly degenerates into a shouting match, which embarrasses the audience. Keep calm, smile and be reasonable. An impromptu joke can work wonders. Leave the audience to hush the hecklers. If they persist, the chairman will ask them to leave and in extreme circumstances the audience will help them to go.

All questions should be answered with civility, patience and good humour. Never let any question disturb your outward composure. The more impertinent it is in intent, the more a polite answer will reflect badly on the questioner and well on the speaker.

Part III
TALKS FOR DIFFERENT PURPOSES

TALKS TO DIFFERENT TYPES OF MEETINGS

Business meetings

Talks to business meetings fall into two main categories, within the speaker's own organization to fellow employees and outside the organization to members of the same professional group employed elsewhere.

Within the organization

Of the two, talking within the organization is usually the more difficult. It is often a question of explaining:

the purpose and function of one's own department
its essential role in helping the organization to achieve its goals
the necessity for cooperation in this by other departments and the methods advocated.

Even when the talk is ostensibly to report progress, the speaker may also have to cover one or more of the other aspects. When it is to report lack of progress, they may loom large on the agenda.

Other departments have their own problems and their own ideas on how to solve them. Their representatives may consider time taken to listen to some idiot waffling on about advertising, research and development, personnel, stock recording, credit control and other trivial matters, could be better spent dealing with urgent work of vital importance, especially if this happens to be producing goods or services.

The way to overcome this reluctance is to stress that:

   the advice you are giving will help their departments to fulfil their functions more efficiently (and without abrogating their managerial rights)

   the enhanced prosperity or even the continued existence of the organization depends on their taking action on what you have to say.

If neither of these propositions is true, you should objectively consider whether your speech and your function are necessary.

No manager welcomes an outsider interfering with the running of his department and is predisposed to resent criticism however helpfully intended. The way to introduce, for instance, a study of clerical methods is not to speak to the head of one department and suggest that his clerks are working at between 50 and 80 per cent efficiency. This will antagonize manager and clerks equally. A speech to managers of all departments pointing out the benefits which have been obtained elsewhere in increased efficiency and ease of working with the same number of clerks or less will encourage those with staff or administrative problems to take the initiative in seeking advice.

A talk designed to improve cost consciousness, the proportion of rejects or customers' complaints should concentrate on the departments achieving the greatest success in these fields and the methods by which they attain it. It would be less likely to win friends and influence people by criticizing the departments with the worst record.

There may be cases where all managers are equally dilatory in sending in their monthly returns of some vital information so that it is not possible to deal with the subject in terms of positive achievement. Even if there is one shining exception it would be tactless to concentrate on it; the manager concerned would be embarrassed if not ostracized. Instead the speaker should concentrate on the fault, its implications for the organization and the positive steps to be taken to remedy it, not on those responsible for causing it. Never indulge in carping criticism.

The same technique is advised when advocating new procedures necessitated by a change in conditions outside the organization, perhaps by a change in the law. The positive approach is again to stress the reasons for the internal change and the methods by which the required results can be achieved.

At meetings within the organization visual aids are often advisable. If your task is to present a quarterly report on production figures, sales, cash inflow, labour turnover or any other continuous index of organizational well-being, it is easier for you and the audience to follow on charts setting out the situation over a period of time and updated for the occasion. The comparative position can be seen at a glance. The audience is reassured by familiar figures which it has already learned to interpret and can question in

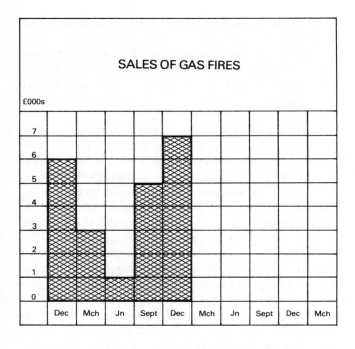

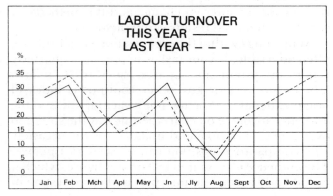

an intelligent way. Points can easily be made about the effects of inflation, price controls, the date of Easter and the works' close-down, the labour market or unseasonable weather.

If the purpose of the talk is to institute a new procedure or to improve the carrying out of an existing one, it is essential that the audience should understand the correct method and be able to implement it properly. After the reasons have been explained and accepted, the procedure should be explained in words of one syllable and discussed until it is clear that it has been clearly understood.

The words must be easy for the particular audience to understand. When talking to fellow employees it is reasonable to use terms fully understood within the organization though not necessarily in the great world outside. BF is recognized in one company as meaning 'brought forward' and has no other implications in personnel records.

The audience should be given a set of written instructions or a checklist for reference when the talk has been partly or wholly forgotten. These are also indispensable for ensuring that instructions passed on by members of the audience to subordinates or others concerned in putting them into effect are not distorted out of recognition. As motives may also be misinterpreted, this handout might start with a short statement on the reasons for the change.

As in the talk, examples should be incorporated showing exactly how the new procedure will work in practice:

Redundancy payments
Employees made redundant will receive two weeks'

average pay for every complete year's service up to and including age 40 and three weeks' pay for every complete year's service from age 41 to state retirement age. These payments will include any state benefit.

Examples

An employee aged 42 with 24 years' service will get 49 weeks' average pay ie

2 weeks' pay × 23 (years' service from age 18 to 40)		= 46 weeks
3 weeks' pay × 1 (years' service from age 41 to 42)		= 3 weeks
	Total	= 49 weeks

An employee aged 58 with 35 years' service will get 87 weeks' average pay ie

2 weeks' pay × 18 (years' service from age 23 to 40)		= 36 weeks
3 weeks' pay × 17 (years' service from 41 to 58)		= 51 weeks
	Total	= 87 weeks

However lucid the written instructions, do not yield to the temptation of believing that they will be sufficient to get a new procedure understood and implemented without a talk. It is quite possible to send a circular to all those concerned but

- you cannot be sure that all of them will receive it, especially if this is later denied
- if they receive it, you cannot be sure that it will be read
- if it is read, you cannot hope that it will be universally understood.

Outside the organization

Business speeches outside the speaker's organization are often given to audiences composed of members of the same or a similar professional group. In this case a great deal of common academic knowledge can be assumed and an understanding of professional terms in general use. If there is any possibility of ambiguity, the speaker should define his meaning of the term precisely.

The main pitfall to avoid is the specialized use within your own organization of a generally accepted term. Inflation accounting is a concept familiar to all accountants but the details of its application may vary considerably from one organization to another.

Finding common ground with everyone in the audience is no problem. All members are more than likely to be interested in their own specialism and will be prepared to listen with avid attention to erudite expositions that would bore the general populace stiff. They will be bored only by being given a great deal of elementary information that they already know.

There is a slight danger of pitching the talk above the heads even of other learned persons. In his novel *A Memorial Service*, (Victor Gollancz, 1976), J I M Stewart describes a paper read by an elderly scholar to an audience of distinguished Oxford dons from mixed disciplines. His theme was the order in which Shakespeare's 154 sonnets must be rearranged in order to disclose the poet's original intention. It was reasonable to rely on the audience's familiarity with the sonnets, said Stewart, 'This venerable scholar, however, owned a faith in us more robust than that, and proceeded on the assumption that he had only to give the number of an individual sonnet to recall it *in toto* to our minds. The postulate conduced to mental fatigue and, I am afraid, inattention.' It is worth noting that those who fell asleep 'had the good manners not to snore'.

Try to ascertain the level of expertise among the audience beforehand. If the group meets regularly and you can attend one or more meetings, this is no problem. If you are unable to get reliable information before speaking, play for safety by making the speech easier to understand than you believe to be strictly necessary. The expressions on faces in the audience while you are talking will indicate whether you need to trade up.

The subject matter for these talks should be prepared with even greater thoroughness than usual. Every point must be checked, every opinion supported. No quarter will be given for slipshod material. Questions will be searching and detailed. Discussion may range far and wide over the whole professional area or subject a minor matter to microscopic examination.

No one would undertake a talk of this kind without sound basic and theoretical knowledge. The audience will expect to enlarge its existing store of knowledge and will be anxious to learn from the speaker's experience. Go prepared with all possible information relating to your own organization's practice and the lessons learned from it.

Make sure you know why certain practices are adopted and others condemned by your own superiors. To experts in other organizations it sounds feeble as well as disloyal for a speaker to say 'I entirely agree that the figures should be kept in the form you suggest but my boss will not allow it.'

On the other hand, do not adopt an attitude so defensive that it excludes consideration of other points of view. The other experts will probably be burning to tell you and the rest of the audience about their own tribulations and successes with certain techniques.

If the audience then displays instant comprehension of every point and members express impatience to press on by shifting in their seats, leaning forward, nodding vigorously and exhibiting other easily interpreted forms of behaviour, speed up delivery and omit some of the simpler or repeated illustrations in order to leave more time for questions and discussion.

At these meetings it is customary to keep the set talk short, often to serve merely as an introduction to the general discussion which forms the major part of the proceedings. Sometimes everyone present is expected to speak briefly about the practice in his own organization. Whatever the formal plan of the meeting, ample time should be set aside for audience participation.

The presentation can be simple and direct, as the audience is unlikely to be swept off its feet by inspired rhetoric. This is no excuse for making it dull. Listeners should not be expected to strain their ears nor to struggle against the desire to sleep, however priceless the pearls of wisdom being proffered.

A speaker expert in his subject is well able to judge what will interest, please and amuse his peers and should strive to make the speech a pleasure to listen to. Instruction of the most sober kind can be enlivened by appropriate illustrations, humorous anecdotes and examples taken from the rich fund of human experience. Learning should not be a painful process. Moreover there are nowadays so many different and agreeable ways of obtaining information that it is almost an insult to offer busy people a boring talk.

Specialist clubs and societies

If you are asked to speak as an expert to a learned society or to a club formed to cater for a common interest among a group, the principles to follow are

practically the same as for a business meeting outside the organization:

much common knowledge can be assumed
specialized terms will be generally understood
the subject matter should:

be comprehensive over the field to be covered

avoid what is elementary and obvious without
being incomprehensibly erudite

include new material from your own research or
experience or a different interpretation of
accepted facts

be thoroughly verified

opinions should be supported by factual evidence

presentation need not be a masterpiece of rhetoric
but should be enlivened with apt illustrations

plenty of time should be allowed for discussion
after the speech.

Visual and aural aids can be important if not essential
to some talks of this kind. Pictures of Alpine meadow
flowers on films, slides and epidiascopes give a truer
and more satisfying account of their colours and
variety than the most skilful words. The cry of the
jackal is more lifelike on record than in any human
imitation.

Talks to geographers or social historians about far
away places with strange sounding customs come to
life through photographs. Talks to music societies
cry out for sound effects. Sometimes these can be
played on an instrument or sung but records and
tapes are more often used.

When you wish to illustrate your talk with sound
effects, it is worth considering recording just the
extracts you want in the sequence required on a
single tape. This saves carrying a pile of records or
tapes and trying at various points in the talk to locate
the exact place at which you wish to pick up the
music or other sound. Then all you need to do is to
indicate in the script when you wish to play an
illustration and switch on. This is less nerve wracking

for the speaker and less distracting for the listeners. When you have promised them the exquisite slow movement from a Mozart symphony or the song of a nightingale, they should not be surprised by the brisk allegro or the corncrake immediately preceding it.

Obviously any speaker wishing to use sound aids would check that the necessary equipment was available or could be transported to the meeting place. Club rooms are frequently less palatial than facilities provided for business meetings. One player who brought his harpsichord to a local factory, confidently expecting to play in the assembly hall on the ground floor, was horrified to discover that the meeting was in a committee room two floors up and served by a small passenger lift.

It is not enough to ascertain, for instance, whether a piano will be available. If you intend to use it, play on it in private. You may find it is more suitable to honky-tonk blues than Debussy or that the pedals complain loudly when pressed down.

Non-specialist groups

Speaking to groups whose only link may be that they all live in Kings Castle and enjoy listening to a good talk once a fortnight demands a quite different approach. The organizer must believe that most members have some potential interest in the work of a bank manager or a probation officer if he invites those officials to speak. It can also be assumed that those without any interest in the topic whatsoever or too deep a personal involvement will stay away or leave after the preliminary cup of tea and raffle.

Some members of the audience will have only the haziest notion about the subject of the talk. Others will hold strong views, possibly erroneous and/or based on false premises. The speaker's main task is to present basic information, dispel ignorance and correct common misapprehensions in an entertaining, universally comprehensible manner.

Start from common knowledge and experience. Everyone knows what a bank looks like; everyone has views on juvenile delinquency. Some listeners will have a bank account or a difficult adolescent child. Few will know the range of services on a personal and a national scale offered by banks and the probation service and their respective success rates.

Progress in easy stages from the known to the unknown and keep on relating concepts and statistics to case histories (anonymous of course in both these instances).

This is not an occasion for breaking new ground, putting out revolutionary ideas or examining any branch of the subject in detail. Technical terms and jargon should be avoided at all costs. Administrative tribulations should not be described unless they relate to the audience's experience. Members might be interested to know, for instance, why banks work apparently short and inconvenient hours or why Billy from the village had to be sent to a special school 100 miles away instead of the one in the next town.

A broad picture should be painted, highlighting all the major points. There is human drama in a bank manager's daily round and there are financial restraints on social work. The whole presentation should give an accurate, though simplified, general impression. It would be inexcusably misleading to foster the view that banks exist only to advance money to deserving individuals or that every client of a probation officer, after one sympathetic counselling session a week, turns into an active supporter of worthy causes, routine drudgery and aged aunts.

Some first rate presentations devised for non-specialist groups combine different techniques to develop one theme. For instance, colour slides of Scotland are shown to the music of Mendelssohn's *Hebridean Overture* and readings of Robert Burns' poetry. By changing the emphasis on different aspects, this presentation can be given to the Holidays at Home group, the Friends of Scotland, the Burns Society, the Music Club, the Townswomen's Guild and the Pensioners' Association.

Social occasions

Honouring the guest
Making a speech on social occasions is similar in many ways to making a vote of thanks (*see* p. 116). The occasion might be the resignation of a club secretary after five years in office or a long service party for all those hardy and persistent enough to have worked 30 years in the same company. The basic requirement is a pleasant, light hearted speech, thanking and where appropriate congratulating the guest(s) of honour.

Such a speech is longer and easier to prepare and deliver than a vote of thanks. As the chief speech of the occasion it can be prepared completely in advance and delivered from notes, if necessary, although it should be presented in as impromptu a manner as possible. The ideal delivery is friendly, relaxed and humorous, with reference only to a few original documents.

The subject matter is easy to define but may need

research. If there is only one guest of honour whose retirement or long service anniversary the speech is to celebrate, it consists mainly of the highlights of his tenure of office. He may or may not have been solely responsible for shaping the events described but any praiseworthy part he played should be noted (needless to say, no jarring note of criticism should be struck on what is essentially a festive occasion). If the person concerned was once a junior clerk filling inkwells at the time when King George and Queen Mary visited the factory, this in itself will arouse pleasant memories of his youth and interest the rest of the audience. His employment record card and personal folder (if available) will yield not only his career pattern but often the material for exercising kindly humour. Boys taken on for the Christmas rush to hold the horse's head on the delivery waggon, and described on their application forms as fit for temporary employment only, often retire 50 years later. Office boys castigated for lacking ambition or not knowing their place rise to divisional manager.

Personnel departments which are understandably reluctant to release personal records can often be persuaded to compile a list of such highlights. Failing personnel records, draw on your own memory and those of others who have known the guest of honour at various stages in his career, selecting suitable incidents from the more scabrous.

The official records of the whole organization are a fruitful source of information. The club or society will keep at least minutes and programmes of activities. Organizations hoard an embarrassing number of recorded riches. With any luck there will be house magazines or newsletters picking out newsworthy items for you over the years in question. Annual reports make less titillating reading but provide solid facts which will trigger personal memories.

It should be possible to find plenty of good background material. Relate this as much as you can to the guest of honour. The installation of the first computer recorded in the annual report might have been the reason why he transferred from the Hollerith section to wages office; the first typing training course could have provided him with a wife.

A presentation is usually made on these occasions. Give it with the assurance that it is a token of the respect/affection/regard for the recipient of all those who contributed.

Visual aids are not necessary and rarely used when there is only one guest of honour. But at a long service party for many guests, fascinating slides may be prepared from photographs from the archives. A display of uniforms, products, photographs of 30 or 40 years ago round the reception room is a certain way of getting the party off to a good start.

Guest of honour's reply

The guest of honour or the one chosen to represent a group should be prepared to make a gracious reply. This may be a speech in its own right or a simple expression of thanks. When people have expended time, effort and money to do you honour, the least you can do is to thank them sincerely for their goodwill and intentions.

This remains true whatever your personal opinion may be of the occasion, the speech or the gift. You may hate social gatherings, being the centre of attraction and any public reference to your career or your private life. You may have been tied by financial necessity to a job you found unutterably boring and see your retirement as a merciful release. You may loathe the ornate clock with which you have been presented and had set your heart on a new pair of binoculars. None of this can excuse you from expressing appreciation; you will have to act, if necessary, and act convincingly.

The first essential is to thank all those who have attended, all those who have contributed to the feast and to the present and the speaker. If the whole party has been organized or even paid for entirely by one person (like the bride's father) give him a personal vote of thanks. Similarly anyone who has travelled a long way or surmounted grave difficulties to be present should be singled out for special mention.

Tell everyone how much you have enjoyed working with them and for them. Thank them for any present, relate it to your known interests and assure them that it will be well used/carefully treasured for ever as a delight in its own right and a reminder of the donors.

This is the minimum. Many occasions call for a full speech. The material for this lies in your career/ tenure of office/years of association with the group. It is sensible to prepare notes of the main events before hand or at least to run over them in your mind. They are sure to correspond in places with the opening speaker's remarks. Similarities can be agreed, errors of fact or interpretation humorously rectified and omissions made good.

Personal reminiscences are the order of the day, ranging from rescuing the present company chairman's toy yacht 40 years ago to the recent fulfilment of a lifetime's ambition to visit the United States on business. These speeches are frankly emotional; try not to let them become sentimental.

After dinner
It is a compliment to be asked to give an after dinner speech. The main qualification is usually that the speaker is known or reputed to speak well and amusingly. As the speech tends to take place at the end of the day, after a large meal, to an audience relaxed with a drink or two, it needs to be.

The best after dinner speakers keep guests rolling in the aisles, not just by what they say but by their droll way of expressing themselves. The old story of the idle undergraduate whose tutor wrote on a reference 'Any company which gets Mr Smith to work for it will be fortunate' needs to be heard in context to extract the full flavour.

The after dinner speaker is not expected merely to tell a string of unrelated jokes. The speech still needs a main theme, which the anecdotes entertainingly illustrate. The theme should be suitable for light treatment and relevant to the interests of the audience. You might be asked to speak at a medical practitioners' dinner on the difficulties confronting a ship's doctor. It is unlikely that the subject would be *New Methods of Controlling Parkinson's Disease* but if it is get it changed.

As with preparation for any other speech, once you have agreed the subject and title the first step is to collect material. Books of stories are published specifically for after dinner speakers. The trouble with them is that many other people will have read them and some may possibly be in the audience.

The best source of material is once again from your own experience. Not a week passes without its share of funny incidents. Some are bound to be funnier than others and some are funny only in the context in which they occur. These can still be used if the speech sketches in the general background.

Some of the best material is funny not as isolated incidents but because of their cumulative effect. As Oscar Wilde pointed out, to lose one parent is a tragedy, to lose both savours of carelessness.

At an industrial tribunal a manager described in detail, and by quoting the exact words, how one of his subordinates had tried to force his way back into the factory at the head of three friends after spending twice the usual lunch hour in a local hostelry and admitting to six Guinnesses and two or three brandies. When restrained at the entrance (on justifiable grounds of endangering his own and others' safety), he called the manager an arrant coward, cast doubts on his mother's honour and threatened to render him unfit for family life. In his defence it was said 'But he was only acting as a shop steward.'

A collection of personal reminiscences is worth its weight in gold to the after dinner speaker. The same general knowledge test mentioned previously produced:

Q With what country do you associate General Smuts?
A The Black Country.
Q How many are there in a quartet?
A Four pints.

With its demise, a light went out in the recruitment office.

When personal experience fails to provide enough suitable material, the public library is again a fruitful source of specialized humour. The section in which to browse is not the one labelled HUMOUR but the one concerned with your subject. If your subject is music, for instance, riffle through biographies of singers, instrumentalists and conductors and you will find a wealth of humour. Gerald Moore and Sir Thomas Beecham alone would enable you to sail through a lifetime of after dinner speeches.

The after dinner speech is not a vehicle for displaying erudition or making weighty pronouncements or developing any subject in minute detail. It is sufficient to have a coherent line of argument so that the theme unfolds logically, and essential to be entertaining.

THE SPEECH AS A TEST

Giving a speech sometimes forms part of an extended selection procedure, either for graduate (or equivalent) entry into a large organization or for promotion to a senior grade. The speech is usually short, perhaps 10 minutes prepared or five minutes virtually unprepared. If the topic is set, the previous advice for gathering material applies but be doubly sure:

   the facts are accurate
   opinions can be supported by evidence.

When all participants are set the same subject, it may well be for an unprepared speech. In this event the longest time available for brooding over it may be from the end of the after dinner discussion to breakfast the next morning. No rational selector expects a well-researched, well-rehearsed performance or even a great depth of knowledge. The topics have to be broad enough to give everyone an equal chance and capable of a variety of interpretations, such as *The Role of Charitable Organizations in Society* or *The Rights of Minorities*.

   Speakers are not expected to produce startling

new theories or have committed reams of statistics to memory. The test is to see whether you can:

approach the subject in a methodical way
develop a line of argument logically to a reasonable conclusion.

It is not of great concern whether you conclude that Dr Barnado's and the Royal Society for the Protection of Birds provide an invaluable outlet for the charitable impulses of individuals or should be nationalized. What matters is that your thoughts should be coherently marshalled, support your argument and be sympathetically expressed in clear, comprehensible English.

Paradoxically a prepared speech set as a test is a more difficult assignment, especially if you are given a free choice of subject with some general proviso that it should be something about which you feel strongly.

Here the choice of subject is crucial. Some topics which undoubtedly engender strong emotion are too vast to encompass in five minutes (war, religious experience). Some about which you may feel strongly (spiders, toy soldiers) might not seem sufficiently weighty to others. Some may offend the selectors. A graduate applicant who addressed a panel all of whose members belonged to the county naturalists' trust and the Royal Society for the Protection of Birds on the joys of shooting wild geese in the Fens failed to get a further interview.

When you have selected a suitable topic, show in the speech that you:

have thought deeply about it
have some worthwhile opinions and original views

can express your thoughts clearly

can sustain attention without placing a strain on the audience for the allotted time.

Whether the speech is prepared or unprepared, try to present it in a way which will make it stand out from the other speeches and therefore memorable. Making deliberately provocative statements will achieve this without having the desired effect of gaining entry/promotion unless it can be demonstrated that they shed new light on old maxims or are an equally acceptable interpretation of the facts. The solemnity of the occasion should not drive out any spark of humour. The adjudicators are likely to welcome some light relief during the eleventh repetition of the same speech, not to mention the rest of the audience.

Whatever the time span, make sure you use it to the full to make as comprehensive a speech as possible and get in all your main points. To state or imply that you have much more interesting material but time has run out is a transparent device.

What is needed is a miniature speech, not a short extract from an hour's address. A plan for a five-minute speech might be:

introduction	one minute
statement of three major issues	three minutes
conclusion	one minute.

INTRODUCTION AND VOTES OF THANKS

How to introduce the speaker

Preliminary courtesies

The organizer of the meeting is responsible for compiling the programme. On most occasions this consists simply of an introduction to the speaker, the speech and a vote of thanks. Sometimes there are several speakers, either giving separate talks or taking part in a discussion. Written programmes are then usually produced. As a matter of courtesy names should be correctly spelled and all speakers should be billed in the same style:

NOT:	2 00pm Mr I Ownett	Managing Director
	2 30pm Jim Whistler	Shop Steward
BUT:	2 00pm Mr I Ownett	Managing Director
	2 30pm Mr J Whistler	Shop Steward
OR	2 00pm Ivor Ownett	Managing Director
	2 30pm James Whistler	Shop Steward

On some programmes it may be deemed desirable to disclose academic and professional qualifications, for example at a learned symposium (to demonstrate credentials) or even at a careers convention for school-leavers (presumably to demonstrate that passing examinations pays dividends in getting a good job). Here again every person whose name appears should be treated equally. Not every speaker or chairman may have the right to append MA, DD, B Mus, Ch M, AMICE and so on after his name but everyone should be told that this is how the programme will be devised and asked to provide any relevant information. It is sometimes assumed that speakers from commerce and industry are unqualified by definition.

Where they are irrelevant, when there is no time to check or the head of the department feels his junior assistant's PhD (Cantab) makes an invidious distinction, academic qualifications are better omitted.

The organizer should also ascertain the rank of members of the audience, so that they may be addressed correctly. An audience is usually a straightforward collection of *ladies and gentlemen*. Even here difficulties seem to arise when there is one woman and several men. Opening speakers have at times been so astounded by seeing one woman in the audience that they have said 'Good morning all' or plunged straight into their introductory remarks without preamble. This is not recommended. It is even worse to fail to notice one or two women scattered about the room and begin 'Gentlemen'. The conventional opening is 'Ladies and gentlemen' even though only one of either sex may be present. In any case there may be others whose stylish crops and

tailored suits or curls and pink shirts make
them more difficult to discern at first sight.

Getting information

Information about well-known speakers may be
gleaned from *Who's Who* or notes about the author on
the covers of books he has written. Sometimes all you
know about your speaker is that he has been recommended to give a talk on edible fungi by someone
who can tell a mushroom from a toadstool. In either
case it is advisable to ask him for personal details.
Aspects of the speaker's career and leisure-time
activities of direct relevance to the speech may have
been omitted from the works of reference. Some which
may have been mentioned may be unwanted.

Speakers tend to be surprisingly modest about
their achievements. Simply writing and asking for
information is likely to produce a scanty brief. More
details will be supplied in answer to specific questions
on, for example, education, academic qualifications,
posts held, hobbies, publications, military service. If
you hesitate to confront the speaker with a bald list of
questions, frame them in a more guarded way: 'I
believe you went from Harrow/Dogpool Elementary
School to the West Indies/Magdalen College to study
botany.'

When you have acquired the facts you need, check
with the speaker what you intend to say. Misinter-
pretation is a danger. 'I spent some years on the
production side at Satanic Mills' might mean 'For 20
years I was managing director' or 'For four years I
worked on a loom'.

Even when the authenticity of the information is
beyond question, it is still necessary to let the speaker

know you intend to divulge it. Some people are adamant about having their war record known, whether this includes being awarded the Victoria Cross or six years in the Home Guard. If the speaker wants anything left out, leave it out. You do not want him to be in any way upset before speaking.

For the same reason, as well as out of courtesy, nothing should be recounted to his discredit. It is unnecessary to say he has travelled by train because he has been debarred from driving for drunkenness. The only occasion on which this might conceivably

113

be relevant is when he is speaking to a group of alcoholics anonymous as a current teetotaller. Even then it is preferable to allow him to make the disclosure himself.

Any necessary domestic announcements, from apologies for absence to apologies for the draughts, should be firmly and completely dealt with before starting to introduce the speaker.

The introduction
It is the clear duty of the chairman of the meeting or anyone else who has to introduce the speaker to remember his name. It is unconvincing to open a meeting with 'Ladies and gentlemen, I am proud to introduce the world famous authority on astrology Mr — er' (quick look at the programme) 'Dr Mooney'. Even chairmen who know the speaker's name well seem compelled to consult their notes at times before daring to utter it because of nervousness or force of habit.

The temptation should be overcome. Get used to using his name even if this means addressing him by it in every sentence exchanged before the meeting opens:

Good evening, Dr Mooney.
Dr Mooney, did you have any trouble finding us?
Please tell me, Dr Mooney, where you would like
   the lectern.

If the speaker happens to be a member of the aristocracy, a bishop, a high-ranking policeman or anyone else with a title, be sure you know the proper form of address and use it clearly so that the audience also gets it right. On the best authority 'In speech, a

Lieutenant-Commander is addressed as *Commander*, a Lieutenant in the Army as *Mr.*'*

The tone of the introduction should be pleasant and friendly but not over-familiar. You may meet the speaker for a drink in the club house every Sunday morning but it is unlikely that he will be on such intimate terms with all members of the audience. A dear-old-George approach may cause some to feel excluded from the charmed circle as well as embarrassing George. On a formal occasion a certain formality should be observed.

The introduction should be as brief as is consistent with recounting the relevant information and making the speaker feel welcome and respected. It may take two minutes and should not exceed five. The audience came to hear his speech, not a talk about him.

There is no need to talk about the subject apart from giving its title. The speaker should do that. Do not anticipate the speech in any way, especially by relating a current joke about it. It may be an intended part of the speech.

You need to know enough about the subject, of course, not to drop any bricks. Philip Hope-Wallace† tells the story of a lecture he gave on Keats soon after the war to a group of servicemen in the canal zone of Egypt. A sergeant major urged them to look attentive and be grateful that a civilian lecturer should come across the desert for their benefit. When he was an ignorant recruit, he said, he did not even know what a keat was.

* *Noblesse Oblige,* edited by Nancy Mitford, Hamish Hamilton Library, reprinted 1973

† In *The Guardian,* 20 January 1979

Introducing the speaker should not be referred to as a chore even obliquely. 'It gives me great pleasure to introduce . . .' is better than 'It gives my task/duty/obligation to introduce . . .' however pleasantly this opening continues.

Make it clear to the speaker when you have come to the end of your introductory remarks. If you have discussed the content with him beforehand, he will have a good idea when you have run through it. You may well add some laudatory sentiment. Then turn to him with a smile and say something like '. . . and we look forward to hearing the expert opinion of Dr Mooney'. Some gatherings clap gently at this point, in which case lead the applause. One of the speaker's horrors is for a lone member of the audience to start clapping and for the sound to die away in a deepening silence.

How to give a vote of thanks
Giving a vote of thanks is more difficult than introducing the speaker. Once the introduction has been made, the introducer can sink back with relief and enjoy or mentally tear to shreds the speech that follows. As he is usually on a seat facing the audience, he must look attentive at all times but his imagination is free to wander. The giver of the vote of thanks needs to concentrate continuously on what is being said.

The introduction can be prepared entirely beforehand and agreed with the speaker. The vote of thanks can only be partly prepared and the speaker can hardly be asked in advance to approve its content.

Optimism is the keynote of the introduction. It can always be understood that the speaker is an expert in the subject and expected that the speech will be a model of clarity and a mine of information. When the time comes to give a vote of thanks, it may be undeniably clear that none of these expectations has been fulfilled. Nevertheless thanks must be given.

Preparation

A certain amount of preparation can be done. If you are called upon to thank the speaker, you will know who he is, what he is speaking about and presumably something about the subject. Find out from the introducer what personal details he has obtained and whether he does not intend to use any which might be helpful to you. If you have a Pooh-Bah role of chairman, secretary and general convenor of the meeting and are introducing and thanking the speaker, this is easy. Otherwise strike a bargain: 'You deal with his honorary degree and I'll mention his research in New Guinea.'

Any previous address by the speaker to the group provides material: 'Since Dr Mooney described so vividly last March the possible effects of the conjunction of Pisces and Venus I have looked forward to hearing him on the forces that caused Napoleon and Hitler to attack Russia.' From experience you may be fairly sure that he will be entertaining/ instructive/stimulating and frame a few sentences accordingly.

If he has never spoken to the group before and was good, you might say: 'It is a joy to discover a new speaker with as fresh and revealing an insight into the causes of economic instability.'

Except on the rare occasions when you are fortunate enough to be sent a typescript of the speech in advance, the amount that can be prepared beforehand is limited. Most of the vote of thanks must be compiled during the speech.

Points from the speech
The vote of thanks should be related to the actual speech, which must be listened to with sympathetic, critical attention; critical because part of the vote of thanks should be a realistic personal assessment of the speech; sympathetic because the assessment should always be expressed in favourable terms. It is essential to be as truthful as possible. Stick to the truth and nothing but the truth but not necessarily the whole truth.

When the speech has been good, there is no problem. Praise should be unstinting. If it was a lucid, witty, masterly exposition of the subject, say so. If it was patchy, dwell on the good parts. A dull exposition of erudite material should be commended for its content, a brilliant delivery of commonplace knowledge for its style.

Mention one or two points of interest in the speech: 'We were particularly impressed by the statistics supporting your theory that red-headed women make the best marmalade,' or 'We all enjoyed your account of the entrepreneur and the tax inspector.'

Votes of thanks are difficult on the rare occasions when you believe the whole speech has been a waste of everybody's time. Even so, something complimentary must be said. You are speaking on behalf of the whole audience and it is amazing how some people can derive benefit and even pleasure from what appears to others as a boring recital of irrelevant information. Apart from this, the audience feels

118

sympathetic towards a thoroughly inept speaker and natural kindness demands courteous treatment.

At the very least the speaker has given up time and taken trouble to prepare the speech and attend the meeting. The delivery may have caused him some anguish. At least send him away feeling that the effort was worthwhile.

It is possible to find something charitable to say about practically anything. For example, a speech which went into every boring detail might be variously described as:

thorough
painstaking
erudite
exhaustive.

One in which the speaker showed a disdain for accepted knowledge and based his opinions on prejudice rather than fact might be considered:

original
thought-provoking
enthusiastic

and so forth.

Your inescapable duty is to sound sincere and appreciative through not less than five sentences. Just to say 'Thank you Dr Mooney for that remarkable speech' is not enough. However little material you may feel you have to work on, avoid obvious padding. This is not the time to tell anecdotes about yourself or members of your family or to repeat the speech, even in part. The audience has already heard it, for good or ill. However much information has been omitted, do not make a speech of your own. The audience will be champing at the bit. If you are more expert than the speaker, you may well be given the chance to cover the ground more adequately at another meeting.

It is quite possible to reach the target by the means described and a concluding remark without padding of this kind.

If the speech had a practical aim, express your belief that it will be fulfilled. 'We shall do our best in the Bottling Plant to reduce our labour turnover to 40 per cent by adopting the techniques you have so ably demonstrated,' or 'This stirring speech will encourage many of us to join the Barset Cockroach Preservation Society straight away.' But be careful not to sound condescending or to have your tongue in your cheek.

Expressing thanks is an occasion on which written notes should not be used. This makes the most genuine tribute appear less sincere. By all means have the basic information you need written down and make notes if you wish during the speech. No speaker objects to such flattering attention. But when you stand up to speak, do not refer to them except in dire necessity. Then act not as if you had run out of pleasant things to say but as if you were referring back to the speaker's exact (and extremely apposite) words.

In short, all votes of thanks should be as brief as is consistent with expressing sincere gratitude. All the blushing speaker needs to do is to smile and say 'Thank you very much.'

Forthcoming attractions
After making a speech, the speaker should continue to

be the focus of attention until the end of the meeting or his particular session in a programme. Domestic notices and announcements, particularly about forthcoming meetings, form no part of a vote of thanks. If they must be made, it is better to make them at the beginning of the meeting. Then all extraneous matters are dealt with before the speaker is introduced and nothing detracts from his performance.

If some domestic crisis occurs during the meeting, draw the whole business to a close and get someone else to make the unavoidable announcement. The secretary might be asked to tell the audience: 'Just before you go, ladies and gentlemen, may I tell you that luncheon has now been prepared in the staff canteen as the marquee has sprung a leak.'

Horror tales related by speakers about announcements that they have kindly agreed to charge no fee and therefore it will be possible to engage a really good professional next time must surely be untrue. It is not unknown, however, for club secretaries to try to whip up enthusiasm for the next speaker by a glowing trailer. Avoid this in the presence of the current speaker. If necessary a conspicuous notice about future meetings can be pinned to a board by the exit or individual notices placed on every chair (except the speaker's) before the meeting.

Examples

Local history lecture
Doctor Emeritus, I know that every member of the Avehenge Historical Society present this evening would wish me to thank you most sincerely for your scholarly account of the development of this area

from Neolithic to Norman times. You have packed so much information into this all too short session that we could draw from it enough subjects for research to occupy us for many years.

The aerial photographs were particularly enlightening. The number of variety of round barrows they revealed was astounding. Some of them were actually unknown to us and warrant investigating as soon as permission can be obtained.

The photographs also provided ample evidence to support your ingenious theory of ancient field boundary systems. The course of old walls and ditches, which could previously be only surmized, was made clearly visible. We shall certainly take advantage of your offer to have copies made so that we can carry this study further.

We were particularly interested to hear your account of the discovery of ninth century bills for flour, milk, eggs and honey among the archives of Burnt Cake Manor. The possible significance of your find can hardly be over-rated! It is work of this kind which makes history come alive and your success renews our enthusiasm to pursue our own researches.

Thank you also for the patient and informative way in which you have answered all the questions which could be crammed into the last half-hour. We very much hope that you will be able to find time to speak to us again soon and look forward to continuing the discussion then.

Flower arrangement
Mrs Aster-Rose, on behalf of everyone here I should like to thank you for your fascinating talk on the art of Ikebana. We have been intrigued to see the effects

which could be produced from a few carefully chosen flowers and branches with unusual materials and exquisite containers. In future we shall view bleached driftwood, pebbles and seed heads with different eyes. It was indeed good of you to bring so many examples in order to demonstrate how different arrangements are built up.

The use of colour was intriguing, in solid masses or in subtle shades of the same basic colour, in white and black and neutral shades. We were enabled to appreciate how they complemented and contrasted with different materials and textures and accentuated the rhythms of the large design.

Perhaps the most interesting aspect of the talk, however, was your explanation of the underlying philosophy and the ways in which different designs signify emotional states such as harmony, joy and repose.

This afternoon you have greatly widened our horizons on flower arranging. Ikebana is a far cry from cramming a mixed bunch of wild flowers into a pottery mug! No doubt we shall continue to use this simple method but now we know how beautiful and meaningful sophisticated arrangements can be, we have higher goals at which to aim. Thank you again for all the trouble you have taken to introduce us to this captivating art.

CHECK LIST

Title of speech . . . .
Place of meeting . . . .
Date of meeting . . . .
Time of meeting . . . .
Time of speech   Start . . . . .   Finish . . . . .
Time of questions   Start . . . . .   Finish . . . . .
Method of travel . . . .
Timing of journey . . . .

Audience
Interests . . . .
Age range . . . .
Sex . . . .
Special characteristics . . . .
Expected knowledge of subject . . . .

Material
Is the material tailored to the interests and level of
    knowledge of the audience . . . .?
Is is thoroughly
        researched . . . .
        checked . . . .

124

sufficient for the speech without overloading
it . . . .
graded for importance . . . .?
Does it cover all the main aspects . . . .
all likely questions . . . .?
Are all direct quotations and quoted views accurate
and fully identified . . . .?

Framework
is the speech well balanced? . . . .
Does it have
an introduction . . . .
development section(s) . . . .
a conclusion . . . .?
Is the line of argument logical . . . .?

Timing
Have you tried out the speech verbally to ensure that
it will fit exactly the time allotted . . . .?
Have you clearly identified material which can be
omitted or inserted as necessary while you
speak . . . .?
Can you see a clock from where you will
stand . . . .?
Is your watch in working order . . . .?

Memory aids
Have you prepared the memory aids you need
typescript . . . .
full notes . . . .
brief notes . . . .
cards . . . .
charts . . . .
slides . . . .?

Visual aids

Are the visual and aural aids you need prepared or
    available in the lecture hall eg

> blackboard, chalk and eraser . . . .
> easel . . . .
> flip charts . . . .
> stiff charts . . . .
> slides . . . .
> films . . . .
> projector . . . .
> epidiascope . . . .
> record player . . . .
> tapes . . . .?

Are they likely to appeal to and be understood by the
    audience . . . .?

How will you transport them . . . .?

Are there enough electrical points of the correct
    voltage . . . .?

Is the system of communication between you and
    any assistant simple and clearly understood on
    both sides . . . .?

Lecture hall

Have you ascertained that the venue is suitable for
    the audience and for the presentation you intend
    to use . . . .?

Seating   —What is the style and arrangement of
                       seats . . . .?

Acoustics—have you tested your audibility in
                       different parts . . . .?
             —have   you   tried   out   the
                       microphone . . . .?
             —can   background   noise   be
                       reduced . . . .?

What is the system of
    temperature control . . . .
    ventilation control . . . .?

Follow up

Did the speech or the questions disclose any gaps in
    your knowledge . . . .?
How are these to be filled? By:

        practical research . . . .
        reading . . . .
        further personal experience . . . .
        investigating   into   the   experience   of
        others . . . .?

Were you clearly heard and understood . . . .?
If not what action needs to be taken to improve
    diction . . . .
    use of language . . . .
    use of microphone . . . .?
Is there any information you have promised to send
    members of the audience . . . .?
Have you made a note of their names and addresses
    . . . .?
Were you
    relaxed . . . .
    confident . . . .
    comfortably dressed . . . .
    competent at dealing with questions . . . .?
If not, what action needs to be taken eg
    more thorough preparation . . . .
    study of relaxing techniques . . . .
    practice before an uncritical audience . . . . . .
    further study of the subject . . . .?

INDEX